Western Hostility to Islam
and Prophecies of Turkish Doom

Western Hostility to Islam

and Prophecies of Turkish Doom

KENNETH M. SETTON

AMERICAN PHILOSOPHICAL SOCIETY
INDEPENDENCE SQUARE: PHILADELPHIA

MEMOIRS OF THE
AMERICAN PHILOSOPHICAL SOCIETY

Held at Philadelphia
for Promoting Useful Knowledge

Volume 201

Library of Congress Catalog Card No.: 91-76984
International Standard Book No.: 0-87169-201-5
US ISSN: 0065-9738

Contents

✳

Preface

This little book was for the most part written some years ago, as indicated at the end of the first footnote, although I have tried to bring it up to date. For a short book I assume that a brief preface is sufficient. There might have been no preface at all except that I must give thanks to my secretary Suki Lewin, on whom I have depended for the Index, and to Carole N. Le Faivre of the editorial board of the American Philosophical Society, who has been responsible for the form and format of the book. For a full half century I have been writing books and articles which some of my critics say are too long and too detailed. The criticism for such books begins with Callimachus, who said that "a big book is like unto a great evil" (μέγα βιβλίον ἴσον τῷ μεγάλῳ κακῷ). But then, some three centuries later, S. Paul observed (in his *Epistle to the Romans, 3.9*) "Let us do evil, that good may come." Both Christians and Moslems have done each other much evil, but for centuries we have waited in vain for some good to come of it all.

1 April 1992   K.M.S.

Early Legends and Prophecies

The tall tales of medieval pilgrims and the incitements of crusading preachers contributed their share to the hatred of Islam nurtured in most Christian hearts during the middle ages. Ridiculous legends grew up in the West relating to Mohammed, the stock in trade of preachers, who were always willing to inform their listeners about the origin of the Prophet and the nature of Islam. Pious Christians were usually assured that Mohammed had come to a bad end. According to one version, he had been eaten by a herd of swine when, one day, he had fallen in a drunken stupor, which made it easy enough for the European (rejoicing in Christianity) to understand why the Moslems rejected wine as well as pork. Mancini has published a composite redaction of the "leggenda di Maometto" (from a Pisan manuscript), with which we may begin as an illustration of the calumny that passed for history until the late Renaissance.[1]

---

[1] Augusto Mancini, "Per lo Studio della leggenda di Maometto in Occidente," *Rendiconti della R. Accademia Nazionale dei Lincei*, Classe di scienze morali, etc., 6th ser., X (Rome, 1934), 325–49. The MS. containing the legend is in the Biblioteca del Seminario di Pisa, Cod. 50. The almost classic account of Mohammed in medieval western thought remains that of Alessandro D'Ancona "La Leggenda di Maometto in Occidente," in the *Giornale storico della letteratura italiana*, XIII (Turin, 1889), 199–281, and cf. the brief essay of L. Bouvat, "Le Prophète Mahomet en Europe, légende et littérature," *Revue du monde musulman*, IX (Paris, 1909), 264–72. On the development of the western attitude toward Islam (to about 1350), see the careful study of Norman Daniel, *Islam and the West: The Making of an Image*, Edinburgh, 1960, and consider also the three essays by R. W. Southern, *Western Views of Islam in the Middle Ages*, Cambridge, Mass., 1962, as well as the various learned (and very readable)

In the days of the apostles a certain Nicolaus, an evil man but one of the seven deacons of Rome, "just as the traitor Judas had been one of Christ's disciples," aspired to the papacy after the death of S. Clement, the third successor of S. Peter. Because of his villainous ways, which included necromancy, Nicolaus was excommunicated by a synod, and imprisoned without food or water in a tower, where he soon died the inglorious death he deserved. Nicolaus's most adept follower was named Maurus, *nefandissimus discipulus*, who disguised himself as a monk and fled from Rome on a ship going to the East. He made his way into Arabia, going up into a mountain at the foot of which lay the chief city of the peninsula. By the preachings of the apostles this city had just been converted to Christianity, and now Maurus took up his residence as a hermit on the mountain which loomed over the city. He became an object of veneration, but burned with the desire to avenge his late master Nicolaus.

One day Maurus saw a boy, *camellos in monte pascens*, whom he called to his side, because he recognized in the boy "through the astronomic art" one to whom he might teach the full measure of his wickedness. Thus Mohammed became the disciple of Maurus, who instructed him in languages and the diabolic arts, and every day Mohammed became more proficient in evil. When the king of the city died without heirs, political dissension ensued. The citizens appealed to Maurus, who had made elaborate plans in anticipation of some such opportunity. By an artful device he contrived the choice of Mohammed as king, and by another "mendacious miracle" secured his acceptance as one especially blessed.

---

works of Bernard Lewis. For the legends and traditions relating to Mohammed in English literature of the later middle ages and the Renaissance, see Samuel C. Chew, *The Crescent and the Rose: Islam and England during the Renaissance*, New York, 1937, esp. pp. 387–434.

This material was originally intended for inclusion in the fourth and final volume of my *Papacy and the Levant*, Philadelphia: American Philosophical Society, 1976–84. It did not, however, easily fit into the chronological and topical structure of any of these volumes, and so (as stated, *ibid.* vol. IV, 1099, note 200) I omitted it. As time passed, I almost forgot it existed, but the recent turmoil (in the Middle East) as well as the increasing Islamic hostility to the West has in strange fashion brought it to life.

The Christian faith was quickly corrupted as Mohammed followed Maurus's abominable and heretical inventions; together they produced a hefty volume, picking and choosing from the Old and New Testaments, but perverting their selections with deliberate obscurity. Thus did Mohammed become the Prophet. In this way was Islam born, with its followers' addiction to a multiplicity of wives and a scandalous degradation of life. Since the Christians made a holiday of Sunday, and the Jews of Saturday, the Moslems chose Friday, "the day of Venus" (*dies Veneris*), obviously most appropriate for their venery (*et merito Venerem colunt qui Veneri idest luxurie incessanter dediti sunt*).

According to this text of the legend, Mohammed, seeking a nocturnal assignation with an unwilling Jewess, was killed by her kinsmen, who cut off his left foot and fed the rest of his body to the swine, *et hec est causa odii inter Saracenos et Iudeos*, and for this reason the Moslems henceforth eschewed pork. Five months after Mohammed's death, when his followers finally located the Jewess, she showed them the left foot she had preserved with salt and unguents. She told them that angels had descended upon the bed where she and Mohammed slept to carry him off (to heaven), but knowing she would have to give an account of what happened, she had held on to his foot in a struggle which had lasted until dawn. Thus the foot had been wrenched from his body, which the angels had carried off, but the Jewess had preserved the foot for the honor of Islam. Now she generously surrendered the foot for proper burial in a sepulcher of adamantine stone, to which thereafter Moslems should make pilgrimage. "And thus their people have increased to the present day, and they hold and venerate and cultivate an iniquitous error."[2]

---

[2] Mancini, *op. cit.* Maurus's master Nicolaus was obviously the founder of the heretical sect of the Nicolaitans. Irenaeus believed him to be one of the seven deacons. Islam was sometimes identified in the middle ages with the "teaching of the Nicolaitans" (Revelation, 2:15), on which cf. D'Ancona, "La Leggenda di Maometto," pp. 245–55, 273, *et alibi*, but was more commonly derived from the Nestorian tradition, which was believed to deny the divinity of Christ (*ibid.*, pp. 229–31, *et alibi*). Note

Some Europeans believed that Moslems worshipped Mohammed as a god, but for the most part he was regarded as a heretic. By the thirteenth century, as we shall see, a good deal was known of Islam, and Vincent of Beauvais collected in his *Speculum historiale* (XXIV, 24–68) many of the legends then current concerning Mohammed. There was a Moslem tradition to the effect that a certain Bahira, a recluse in a Christian monastery at Busra, recognized the young Mohammed as a future prophet or spokesman of God. In other western legends a part similar to that of Maurus (in the Pisan text published by Mancini) is played by one Sergius, in whom Bahira may be recognized. Most westerners had little understanding of Islam. They did not indeed want to understand Islam; they wanted merely to refute it. Contrary to most Christian opinion, the Bible and the Koran (al-Qur'ān) are actually not properly to be compared, at least not from the Moslem standpoint, for Moslems believe the Koran to be the direct and uncreated Word of God. Christians err in their contrast of Christ and Mohammed. No Moslem worships Mohammed, who is only the messenger of God: "the Bible derives its significance from Christ; but Muhammad derives his from the Qur'ān."[3]

While Christian apologists insisted that the Koranic recognition of Christ and confirmation of the Scripture made clear the truth of the Christian Revelation, they also affirmed that the Koranic addition of Mohammed to the prophets obvi-

---

also P. Alphandéry, "Mahomet-Antichrist dans le moyen-âge latin," in the *Mélanges Hartwig Derenbourg*, Paris, 1909, pp. 266, 269, and especially Daniel, *Islam and the West*, pp. 83ff., 234ff. The story of Mohammed's being killed by a Jewess, who retained his left foot, is well known (D'Ancona, "La Leggenda," pp. 249–50, and Daniel, *op cit.*, p. 105), and appears in a seventeenth-century Armenian MS. published by F. Macler, in the *Mélanges H. Derenbourg*, pp. 287–95. S. Pedro Pascual [Petrus Pascasius], bishop of Granada and later of Jaen (1296), helped to popularize the tale in the thirteenth century (D'Ancona, pp. 240ff. and 250, note 1). Pedro Pascual knew, however, a good deal about the Moslems (Ugo Monneret de Villard, *Lo Studio dell' Islām in Europa nel XII e nel XIII secolo*, Città del Vaticano, 1944, pp. 57–58, Studi e testi, vol. 110). There is some question as to the correctness of the attribution to Pascual of the works on Islam which pass under his name.

[3] Daniel, *Islam and the West*, pp. 33, 88–89, 235.

ously invalidated the Koran itself. Rather inconsistently, then, they employed the invalid Koran to illustrate the validity of the Bible, while the fact that the Bible neither foretold nor confirmed the Koran and Mohammed made it quite apparent to Christian apologists that the Moslem Book could not be the Word of God. The Moslem answer was that it was precisely this failure of the Bible, this incompleteness of the Old and New Testaments, which had led God to speak directly to Mohammed through Gabriel the Word which was in fact the Koran. Christian apologists saw in the Koran a pernicious and deceitful confusion of falsity and truth, and when they contrasted Christ with Mohammed, they noted with satisfaction the Moslems' own acknowledgment of "the Islamic Christ alive in Heaven while Muhammad lay admittedly buried in Arabia."[4] The Moslems believed of course in Christ's ultimate acceptance of Islam, but their denial both of his divine nature and of the Christian doctrine of the Trinity earned them the implacable hostility of western writers.

The gift of prophecy was respected and feared in the ancient East, not only among the Hebrews and early Christians. From the later seventh century, in the time of the Umaiyad caliphs, prophecies (especially those based upon certain conjunctions of the planets) exercised much influence upon the conduct of affairs in the Islamic world. Prophecies were mostly of two types. There were, first, more or less specific predictions, usually of unknown origin, which foretold the death of some great person or the occurrence of some important event, and secondly there were whole books of apocalypses about which the Moslems first learned from the Jews and Christians. Most of the prophets in the Islamic world were in fact Jews or Jewish and Christian renegades, converts to Islam, and there was to be no abatement of their visions under the Selchükid and Ottoman Turks. They spun their prophetic webs from their own imaginations, often employing strands from the Bible, especially the Book of Daniel. In the Islamic world *al-jafr* (divination) and *malāḥim* (sing. *malāḥamah*, prophetic poem) took the place of the western

---

[4] Daniel, *op. cit.*, p. 172.

Sibylline *vaticinia*. One of the most frequent forms of prediction in the *malāhim* was to identify persons, things, and
places by single letters: "Qāf will kill Mīm with the aid of
Jīm . . .,"[5] a practice which is said to have persisted until at
least the later nineteenth century.

A large number of extant manuscripts attests to the widespread interest which the prophecies evoked in late medieval
and early modern times, and the apparent belief they inspired among the learned as well as among the ignorant. In
both East and West many prophecies foretold internal devel-
opments of the Moslem and Christian states, but many others
concerned the great contest between Islam and Christianity,
one of the main themes of world history.

We find a notable example in an Islamic prophecy of Egyptian origin, composed in its present form between 1180 and
1220. It relates to the year A. H. 561 (i.e., from November
1165 to October 1166), and reflects with messianic gloom
and grandeur the conflict of East and West in the era of the
early Crusades. This prophecy foretells the drying up of Lake
Tiberias, the burning of Cairo three times, and the enslave-
ment of Egypt. The king of the Khazars was to meet the Turks
five times in battle, and blood would flow like a river. Western armies of great strength, 100,000 men or more, would be
victorious, returning to Egypt for a second time and pitching
their tents between the Turks and Ascalon and Tiberias. . . .
Constantinople would be destroyed. The Antichrist would
appear "for forty days," and Jesus in yellow raiment would
climb the minaret on the east side of Damascus: He would re-
cite prayers for the people, seek out the Antichrist, and slay
him at the gate of Ludd (Lydda). . . . Finally the earth would
deliver up its best to mankind. Christ would marry and beget
children, and when he died, he would be buried at Medina
between Mohammed and Abu-Bakr. God would then send a
gentle breeze beneath His throne. It would lift up believers
under the arms, and carry them away to death. But evil men

[5] G. van Vloten, *Recherches sur la domination arabe, le Chiitisme et
les croyances messianiques sous le khalifat des Omayades*, Amsterdam,
1894, pp. 54ff., 57.

would continue to live until time broke in upon them.[6] Whatever the significance of the various details of the prophecy, the prediction that evil men would live on seems quite justified by the subsequent events of Levantine history.

In the West, from the beginning of the thirteenth century, the prophecies of the Abbot Joachim of Flora were famous, and provided soil for the growth of many Pseudo-Joachimite predictions. More than three centuries of Moslem domination in Sicily and countless raids upon Calabria lay behind the Joachimites' attributing apocalyptic significance to the Saracen danger. The Crusades fastened Europe's attention upon the East, and inspired Christian hopes of victory over Islam. Merlin's fame in medieval legend was such that various prophecies were enunciated in his name. Eastern affairs received emphasis in the prophetic literature of the time, and a Sibylline book of the thirteenth century "foresees" the advent of Mohammed: "Erit autem bestia horribilis ab oriente veniens. . . ."[7]

---

[6] Richard Hartmann, *Eine islamische Apokalypse aus der Kreuzzugs-zeit: Ein Beitrag zur Ğafr-Literatur*, in the Schriften der Königsberger Gelehrten Gesellschaft, Geisteswissenschaftliche Klasse, I-3, Berlin, 1924. On the Moslem concept of Antichrist (Daggal, not named in the Koran), see van Vloten, *Recherches*, pp. 59–60; cf. also A. Abel, in *Arabica*, V (1958), 7, 9, and Guy Le Strange, *Palestine under the Moslems* (1890, repr. Beirut, 1965), pp. 493–94.

[7] O. Holder-Egger, "Italienische Propheten des 13. Jahrhunderts," *Neues Archiv der Gesellschaft für ältere deutsche Geschichtskunde*, XV (Hanover, 1890), 143ff., 162, and cf., *ibid.*, XXX (1905), 331. To Joachim of Flora "the chief instruments of Antichrist were the Saracens" (Southern, *Western Views of Islam*, pp. 40–41). The Joachimist prophecies lasted into the early seventeenth century (cf. Marjorie Reeves, *The Influence of Prophecy in the Later Middle Ages: A Study in Joachimism*, Oxford, 1969, pp. 100–2, 335–37, 348–49, 353, 356, 364, 367–68, 370, 449, *et alibi*).

Prophecies of Islamic doom were frequent in Christian works of the later crusading era. An ardent reader of history and a persistent advocate of the crusade in the later fourteenth century, Philippe de Mézières (1327–1405), chancellor of the kingdom of Cyprus, fervently believed (as his biographer Nicolae Jorga informs us) that "la puissance des Infidèles n'était plus à craindre, malgré leurs victoires. Si leurs armées étaient innombrables, leur organisation solide et leurs possessions étendues, ils étaient à la veille de périr. Dieu les avait condamnés, et ils le savaient eux-mêmes." The Moslems knew of their coming destruction from various "prophéties contemporaines," or at least Philippe de Mézières believed so

The prophet was apparently not without honor, even in his own country, when he could see through the dark clouds of the future to catch a glimpse of disaster. A much-read page in a parchment manuscript of the fourteenth century (now in the Vatican Library) relates what a certain "prophet of Vienne" had to say at the Second Council of Lyon, when he was asked about the future of the Holy Land. According to the *propheta Viennensis*, the kingdom of Jerusalem would soon suffer a change of rule, and what began in discord would end in discord (*quod quidem dominium in discordia inciperet et in discordia finiretur*). The Saracens were harassing the Holy Land. The Tatars, who had appeared at the Council of Lyon (in July 1274), would do nothing for the present, "but soon they would enter the kingdom of Jerusalem and take possession of it . . . the faithful would rejoice in their coming, . . . and finally the Tatars would disappear." The text continues with the assurance that "[the prophet] also said that I who have written these things would see Alexandria in Christian hands, Armenia subject to French rule, and the Greeks scattered throughout the world in exile after their loss of Constantinople." The mysterious prophet foretold some measure of reform among the Hospitallers. The Germans would leave the Holy Land, "et ad debellandos barbaros in septentrione insudabunt." As for the Templars, they would increase in numbers, but decline in virtue. The Franciscans would soon face schism and turmoil, and the

---

(Jorga, *Philippe de Mézières et la croisade au XIVe siècle*, Paris, 1896, p. 30). On Mézières and his participation in the crusade in his time, cf. K. M. Setton, *The Papacy and the Levant (1204–1571)*, 4 vols., 1976–84, I, 236ff., 241, 259–61, 271–73, *et alibi*.

Later on, other prophecies were to foretell the gradual breakdown of Islamic society and the Ottoman Empire as beginning at the millennium of the Hegira, i.e., at the year 1591–1592, in the time of the sultan Murad III (1574–1595), during whose reign in fact the downtrend of Turkish fortunes did begin (cf. H.A.R. Gibb and Harold Brown, *Islamic Society and the West: Islamic Society in the Eighteenth Century*, Oxford University Press, repr. 1963, vol. I, pt. 1, pp. 179ff.). Prophecies of Turkish doom, however, had a far wider currency in the Christian West than in the Islamic East.

Dominicans would seek property rather than learning and letters.[8]

The West was quite as fertile in prophecy as the East. After the death of King Henry V of England in September 1422, war dragged on for years between Charles VII of France and the supporters of the young Henry VI. At some point an unknown scribe in England copied a prophecy ascribed to one Johannes Bessagorii, who was said to have foretold the almost complete annihilation of the French kingdom by invaders in 1420 (in December of which year Henry V had indeed entered Paris). Johannes had also foreseen, however, the even more dreadful disasters which were to come about two years later (*circa annum Domini MCCCCXXII*) when one man would rise up to smite another, cities would fall, desolation would fill the earth, and no one would keep faith with his fellows. The vengeance of the Lord would be over all. The infidels would overrun Europe as well as the Levant. Floods and earthquakes would wreak widespread havoc. Cyprus and Sardinia would be laid waste. The Catalans and Castilians (*Aragones et Hispani*) would wage war until one kingdom or the other had been entirely destroyed. Wherever in fact Johannes Bessagorii cast his baleful eye, he saw almost ineffable ruination. The Turks would destroy many islands in the Aegean, and the Greeks would "invade the realm of the Latins and despoil it completely,"[9] apparently an allusion to the liquidation (by the Palaeologi in 1432) of the old Latin principality of Achaea, which had been established in the Morea after the Fourth Crusade.

An interesting prophecy of a few years later also relates to the Palaeologi. The Moreote Greeks placed their hopes for defense against Turkish invasion in the Hexamilion, the so-called "six-mile" wall across the Isthmus of Corinth, which had been fortified three times in the long past, against the Persians (in 480 B.C.), the Huns (about A.D. 552), and the

---

[8] Bibl. Apost. Vaticana, Cod. lat. 3822, fol. II, *ad initium*.

[9] British Library, Cotton MS., Cleopatra C.IV, 26a, fols. 81–82 [82–83], *Profesia Johannis de Bessagorio:* ". . . Vindicta domini generaliter et specialiter erit super omnes. Turci a latere multas insulas Christianorum destruent. Greci regnum Latinorum invadent et ipsum totum spoliabunt. . . ."

Ottoman Turks (in 1415). The prophecy in question foretold success against the enemy when the Hexamilion (destroyed in May 1423) should be re-erected for the fourth time, "and Justice [Δίκη] will come to the race of Hellenes from heaven, along with good fortune [τύχη], and she will subject to the yoke their former shameless destroyers—most blessed is he who for the fourth time will fortify the isthmus. . . ."[10] In 1443 Constantine [XI] Palaeologus, then despot of the Morea, did rebuild the Hexamilion for the fourth time. In November of the following year, however, Sultan Murad II defeated at Varna the crusading army of John Hunyadi and Ladislas, king of Poland and Hungary, after which there was scant hope of the Greeks' receiving substantial aid from the West. The Turks destroyed the Hexamilion again in 1446, leaving the Palaeologi and the peninsula defenseless against the raids which would lead to the Ottoman occupation of the Morea in 1460. The Isthmian prophecy, probably composed in the early 1430s, was clearly designed as propaganda to encourage Greek resistance to the Turkish advance.

About the beginning of the 1460s, early in the reign of Pope Pius II, a prophecy was produced which provided a very precise timetable for the expected Christian victory over the Turks. This prophecy, which was known to at least some members of the Curia Romana, was allegedly transmitted to the pope by the king of France, Charles VII or Louis XI. The prophecy had, to be sure, an adequately gloomy beginning. The pope would die in 1466, there would be famine in 1467, and all the clergy would perish in 1468. The Turk would put Christendom under siege from Rhodes to Rome in 1469, but the king of France would break the siege of Rome (at the Porta Latina), and force the Turk into flight as far as the Holy Sepulcher in Jerusalem. The Turk in fact would be utterly defeated in 1470, and a hermit elected pope, under whom the Christian world would finally be

---

[10] Edward W. Bodnar, "The Isthmian Fortifications in Oracular Prophecy," *American Journal of Archaeology*, LXIV (1960), 165–71, with full bibliography.

united in 1471. And, having obviously done his part, the king of France was to die the following year.[11]

In the West, Mohammed was sometimes represented as one of the false prophets (to whom Christ referred in Matthew, 24:11), whose appearance would presage the end of the world. Mohammed might even be portrayed as the Antichrist, the second Beast of the Apocalypse, whose "number is six hundred and sixty and six" (Rev. 13:18), which was declared to be the number of years of Moslem sway in the world. Popular preachers could describe the Crusade as the struggle of saints against the Beast. But if Mohammed was castigated as the Antichrist by Alvarus of Cordova in the ninth century, he appeared to Peter the Venerable in the twelfth century rather as the precursor of Antichrist.[12] An unholy trinity would reveal itself in historic sequence—Arius, Mohammed, and Antichrist. By the fourteenth century Arius could be set aside, and the trinity of damnation became Mohammed, Averroës, and Antichrist. For the most part, then, medieval seers and theologians did not identify Mohammed with the Antichrist. Some of them tended rather to see in him, as Dante did in the Inferno (XXVIII, 35), a *seminator di scandalo e di scisma*. A famous and oft-quoted line,

---

[11] Bibl. Apost. Vaticana, Cod. lat. 5994, a fifteenth-century potpourri containing the prophecy in question (fol. 86):

> Sanctissimo domino nostro Pio pape Secundo, transmissum per serenissimum regem Francorum:
>
> Anno 1466. Roma papa carebit.
>
> Anno 1467. Multi fame peribunt.
>
> Anno 1468. Omnis clerus interficietur.
>
> Anno 1469. Obsessio erit per Turchum a Rodio usque Romam per portam latinam, et obsessa Roma rex Francorum Turchum constringet in fugam usque Yerusalem ad Sepulcrum Christi.
>
> Anno 1470. Turchus superatus et victus. Fiet papa quidam heremita. Electus ab angelo sub arbore siccha, missam celeb[r]abit, et tunc arbor illa florebit.
>
> Anno 1471. Tempore ipsius pape fiet unio totius Christianitatis.
>
> Anno 1472. Dehinc rex Francorum morietur.

[12] Cf. Bibliothèque de l'Arsenal, Paris, MS. 1162, fol. 1: ". . . maximus precursor Antichristi et electus discipulus diaboli Mahumet . . ." (cited by Marie-Thérèse d'Alverny, "Deux Traductions latines du Coran au moyen-âge," in *Archives d'histoire doctrinale et littéraire du moyen-âge*, XVI [Années XXII–XXIII, 1947–48], 79).

it summarizes well much of the western attitude toward Mohammed.[13]

Although much nonsense was written about Mohammed and the Moslems in the middle ages, the fact is that from the earlier thirteenth century the Spanish Dominicans could have enlightened their fellow Europeans as to both the man and his doctrine, at least to some extent, but they studied Arabic in their convents in Spain, North Africa, and the Levant for the purpose of refuting, not interpreting Islam. Mostly they studied Arabic to preach the gospel *in partibus infidelium*, not to read the Koran. The Franciscans were no less active in the Levantine missionary movement, but their knowledge of spoken Arabic did not necessarily entail a significant acquaintance with the historical or religious literature of Islam.

Provision was made for the study of Arabic as well as of Greek and Hebrew in the major universities, but actually no linguistic wonders seem to have been accomplished. To be sure, Humbert of Romans demanded of preachers of the Crusade not only some geographical knowledge of the Holy Land, but a direct acquaintance with the Koran and some familiarity with the facts of Mohammed's career. Pierre Dubois, as is well known, also insisted upon a knowledge of oriental languages on the part of the Christian stalwarts who were going to colonize anew the ancient lands of Palestine and Egypt. Some of the Spaniards knew a good deal of Arabic and much about Islamic culture; one thinks of Ramón Martí and S. Pedro Pascual, Arnald of Villanova and Ramón Lull. Important translations were made at Toledo, including one of the Koran (in 1210), as we shall have cause to note later.

Fra Ricoldo da Montecroce (1243–1320) learned much about Islam and the Moslems during his travels in Syria, Persia, and Mesopotamia and his long sojourn at Baghdad, where he may have begun a translation of the Koran. Upon his return to Italy, however, he was more concerned with

---

[13] Cf. P. Alphandéry, "Mahomet-Antichrist dans le moyen-âge latin," in the *Mélanges Hartwig Derenbourg*, Paris, 1909, pp. 261–77, and Daniel, *Islam and the West*, pp. 184–88, 192.

rehearsing the errors of Islam than with attempting to increase understanding between his fellow Christians and the Moslems. Given the temper of the times, this was to be expected. Fra Ricoldo's refutation and vilification of Islam (often called the *Improbatio Alcorani*) was eventually translated into various European vernaculars and was often reprinted in the sixteenth century.[14] In the later thirteenth and earlier fourteenth centuries some westerners, most notably Ramón Martí and Lull, had a considerable knowledge of Islamic theology. But in Europe the study of Arabic, and therefore access to a basic knowledge of Islamic culture, declined markedly after about 1330, not to be revived until the seventeenth century.[15]

---

[14] Cf. Daniel, *Islam and the West, passim.* The printed text of Ricoldo da Montecroce's *Confutatio* or *Improbatio Alcorani* (in *PG* 104) is a Latin version of the Greek translation made by Demetrius Cydones in the late fourteenth century, not in the fifteenth, as stated by Daniel, *op. cit.*, p. 234. The original Latin version of Ricoldo's work remains unpublished.

[15] Ugo Monneret de Villard, *Lo Studio dell' Islām in Europa* (1944), pp. 35–77, and "La Vita, le opere e i viaggi di Frate Ricoldo da Montecroce, O.P.," in *Orientalia Christiana periodica*, X (1944), 227–74, as well as the same author's study of *Il Libro della peregrinazione nelle parti d'Oriente di Frate Ricoldo da Montecroce*, Rome, 1948. In Spain Koranic studies lasted until the close of the fourteenth century (Monneret de Villard, *Lo Studio dell' Islām*, pp. 30–32). The Abbot Peter the Venerable of Cluny in the mid-twelfth century reveals a considerable knowledge of Islam, as we shall note, based upon the Latin translation of the Koran (made for him by Robert of Ketton), the refutation of Moslem doctrine in the *Risālah* or *Apology* attributed to al-Kindī (translated for him by Peter of Toledo), and some other works prepared for him in the "Toledan-Cluniac Collection" (on which see N. Daniel, *Islam and the West, passim*; James Kritzeck, *Peter the Venerable and Islam*, Princeton, 1964, esp. pp. 115ff., in the Princeton Oriental Studies, no. 23; and the fundamental study of Marie-Thérèse d'Alverny, "Deux Traductions latines du Coran au moyen-âge," in *Archives d'histoire doctrinale et littéraire du moyen-âge*, XVI [Paris, 1947–48], 69–131).

Berthold Altaner has identified more than a score of missionaries and scholars in the thirteenth and fourteenth centuries, especially Dominicans, who had a good knowledge of Arabic, and a half dozen others who may have had some knowledge of the language ("Zur Kenntnis des Arabischen im 13. und 14. Jahrhundert," *Orient. Christ. periodica*, II [1936], 437–52). Note also Altaner, "Sprachstudien und Sprachkenntnisse im Dienste der Mission des 13. und 14. Jahrhunderts," in *Zeitschr. für Missionswissenschaft*, XXI (1931), 113–36, and *Die Dominikanermissionen des 13. Jahrhunderts*, Habelschwerdt, 1924, as well as Odulphus van der Vat, *Die*

When the serious study of Islam declined in Europe, the nonsense written about Mohammed was certain to continue. In the late fourteenth century, for example, William Langland furnished readers of his vision of *Piers the Plowman* with an account of Mohammed's career that had received wide currency in earlier generations. To begin with, Mohammed was a Christian, "and a cardinal of court, a gret clerk with-alle" who wanted to become pope, "pryns of holychurche." But he was like a bad penny, says Langland; and there was no place for him in the social economy of Rome. Mohammed therefore made his way into Syria where by wiles and magical arts the Saracens were beguiled into believing he was in direct communication with heaven, and thus it was a false Christian who had founded the false faith which dominated the Levant.[16]

Anfänge der Franziskanermissionen und ihre Weiterentwicklung im nahen Orient und in den mohammedanischen Ländern während des 13. Jahrhunderts, Werl i. W., 1934. Van der Vat says little, however, about the language question. On the Dominican and Franciscan missions in the Levant and the study of the eastern languages, cf. K. M. Setton, "Byzantine Background to the Italian Renaissance," *Proceedings of the American Philosophical Society*, vol. 100 (1956), 18ff., 33ff.

[16] W. W. Skeat, ed., *Vision of William [Langland] concerning Piers the Plowman* . . ., 2 vols., Oxford, 1886, I, 462ff.: B-Text, Passus XV, vv. 389ff., and C-Text, Passus XVIII, vv. 165ff. According to Langland, Mohammed was "lyke a Lussheborgh," i.e., a spurious coin imported into England from Luxembourg. A versified version of Brunetto Latini's *Tesoro* from about the year 1300 also represents Mohammed as *monaco e cardinale* (D'Ancona, "La Leggenda," pp. 199ff., *et passim*). Cf. E. Doutté, *Mahomet Cardinal*, Châlons-sur-Marne, 1889.

Christian Hopes for
the Undoing of Islam

A Moslem tradition which was alleged to go back to Mohammed himself had long maintained that the world would not end nor the last judgment begin until the Greeks (*Rūm*) were converted to Islam and Constantinople had been captured. Such prophecies probably went back to the Umaiyad failures to take the city in the later seventh and early eighth centuries. Islamic (like European) prophecy was often tinged with heretical opinion, and might well have ulterior religious or political motivation, for internecine war and religious dissension were quite as characteristic of Islamic as of European society.

When at long last the Turks did succeed in taking Constantinople, in May 1453, the news was received with horror and foreboding, especially in Rome and Venice. A certain Fra Giovanni Stupan, a Venetian, claimed to have foretold in 1450 the coming fall of the city. He also prophesied a Turkish advance upon Rome as well as other events to befall Venice, the papacy, and the Ottoman empire. Fra Giovanni's prophecies covered a wide range. When his prognostications for the years 1519–1520 (?) remained unfulfilled, some reader of the Vatican manuscript which contains them obligingly altered the dates to 1619–1620.[17] Those who believe in prophecy

_____

[17] Bibl. Apost. Vaticana, Cod. lat. 13,683, fols 1–4ʳ: "In Christo nomine amen. Memoria chome del 1450 fezi prenzipio a questo dire chome el Turcho ad ogni muodo averà Constantinopoli però che leterno dio vuolle dar prinzipio de renovare la soa santa giexia manō tropo tempo driedo Con-

are always anxious to assist the prophet. When they come to regard themselves as divinely chosen instruments to help make a prophecy come true, they may well work with obsessive determination to help bring about the forecast. Islamic society had been haunted for at least six centuries by *hadith* to the effect that Moslems would some day take Constantinople. As time passed, it became increasingly clear to the whole Islamic world that the Ottoman Turks would prove to be the chosen people who should fulfill the prophecy.[18] And toward that end the Turks worked hard.

After the fall of Constantinople the Greeks tormented themselves for years with prophecies of the reconquest of the great city. The Turks also, especially at the lower levels of society, instilled fear into their own hearts by prophecies of a Christian reconquest, which was to come some disastrous Friday during the midday prayer when the Moslem community was gathered in the mosque. The gate by which the Christian return was supposed to be effected was kept walled up, and the gates of Christian quarters in various other towns were closed during the Friday prayers. Time was not to relieve the Turkish sense of foreboding, and the millennium of the *Hijra* (beginning on 19 October 1591) was to prove a period of apprehension among some Moslems. These eastern prophecies were by and large spontaneously born of Greek hope or Turkish fear.

A good deal of western prophecy, however, which foretold the Christian repossession of Constantinople and the destruction of the Ottoman empire was contrived for publicist pur-

---

stantinopolli abiterà lo inperador de Christiani. Item lo Turcho ad ogni modo andarà a Roma et avanti che lui vada el farà una grande e potente armada per mare e per tera et anderà verso el Danubio e li se fortificherà con grande provisione de gente e de munitione azo che Ongari ne altri Christiani non posa pasare ne dare in pazo a Chonstantinopolli." For the alteration of the date, referred to in the text, see, *ibid.*, fol. 4^r.

[18] Cf. Louis Massignon, "Textes prémonitoires et commentaires mystiques relatifs à la prise de Constantinople par les Turcs en 1453 (=858 Hég.)," *Oriens*, VI (1953), 10–17, and cf. Osman Turan, "The Ideal of World Domination among the medieval Turks," *Studia Islamica*, IV (1955), 77–90, who ends his paper with a notice of the "Red Apple," on which see below.

poses, and some of these (later) *vaticinia* and *prophetiae* were probably produced in the chanceries of Charles V and his brother Ferdinand I. They were in fact deliberately manufactured as crusading propaganda, and some of them were destined to enjoy a long life. Fewer anti-Turkish pronouncements of a prophetic nature were of French than of German origin. Traditionally leaders of the Crusade, the French were too often the allies of the Turks from the time of Francis I, who had found an entente with the Porte the best way of counter-balancing the Hapsburg power in Europe.

From the later fourteenth century to the beginning of the twentieth, Europeans tended to identify Islam with the Ottoman empire, especially after the Turks had crushed the Persians (in 1514), and had thereafter overrun eastern Anatolia and Kurdistan (in 1515), Syria and Palestine (in 1516), and finally Egypt in January 1517. Pious Christians must pray for the undoing of Islam. Sometimes biblical texts were recast into anti-Turkish prognostications. The soothsayers could be convinced by the products of their own imagination, and thus be duped by their own ingenuity. There were presumably few free thinkers in the sixteenth century, the *saeculum theologicum*; the mentality of the period was much less critical even than that of our own time. Religion was basic to statecraft, and the Church still wielded the most powerful sanctions. The Crusade was almost the only consistent eastern policy the papacy ever devised, and hostility to the Turk had become almost an article of faith.

Prophecies might be presented with a specificity of fact or date which soon proved them to be erroneous, but then they were assumed merely to have been misdated or misinterpreted. Some of them became in fact *idées-forces* of singular longevity and fertility. It might even be asserted by a doubting Thomas (and there were such) that some of the anti-Turkish prophecies were of Ottoman origin, designed to lure foolhardy Christians into one or another doomed adventure or crusade.[19]

---

[19] Cf. Jean Deny, "Les Pseudo-Prophéties concernant les Turcs au XVIᵉ siècle," *Revue des études islamiques*, X (1936), 201–5.

The Turks did not relish crusades, however, and their propaganda never took the form of trying to entice Christian armies into the East in order to destroy them. As the Turks enjoyed success one generation after another, the Italians, Hungarians, Transylvanians, Germans, and others whose lands were exposed to possible Turkish attack, needed reassuring that eventually the cross would triumph over the crescent. The mendicant preachers often gave them that reassurance. On 31 March 1480, for example, the Dominican friar Giovanni Nanni da Viterbo (1432–1502) addressed a *Tractatus de futuris Christianorum triumphis in Turcos et Saracenos* (printed at Genoa on the following 8 December) to Pope Sixtus IV, the kings of France, Spain, Sicily, and Hungary, and to the government of Genoa. Nanni explored the question whether the prophet Mohammed was really the Antichrist, with learned citation of the works of the Franciscan Nicholas de Lyra, his fellow Dominicans Ramón Martí and Ricoldo da Montecroce, as well as a number of others. The question was finally answered in the affirmative.

Nanni had no doubt that the Christians would recover all the lands they had lost to the Turks. God had predestined the reconquest, which might be achieved by the intervention of Christ or by the exercise of human effort. Nanni's prophecies were drawn from Revelation and buttressed by astrological considerations. The Ottoman empire, he believed, would fall under the seventh sultan, who was identified with the seventh angel in the apocalypse of the bowls of divine wrath (Rev. 16: 17–21). Actually Mehmed II, conqueror of Constantinople, was seventh in the list of Ottoman rulers, of whom the first three did not use the title "sultan." Although this fact is of little moment in the present context, Nanni complicated his prophetic calculations by employing an erroneous list, which showed Mehmed to be the eighth sultan. Since this obviously vitiated his prophecy, Nanni stated that two of the eight sultans had to be disregarded since they had never aspired to the capture of Constantinople. The destruction of the Ottoman empire would thus come in the time of Mehmed II's successor, who would be the true seventh sultan.[20]

Among those to whom Giovanni Nanni had addressed his prophecy of Christian victory over Islam was King Louis XI of France. The French had once been *par excellence* the crusading nation. Louis's successor Charles VIII had been nourished from boyhood on chivalric romances and tales of the East. As he grew older he cast himself in the role of a second Charlemagne, and his Italian expedition in 1494–1495 was not only to claim a kingdom which he asserted belonged

---

[20] Cf. N. Iorga, *Notes et extraits pour servir à l'histoire des croisades*, V (Bucharest, 1915), doc. no. LXXVII, pp. 62–64; Deny, "Les Pseudo-Prophéties," p. 216. The perpetrator of some of the most remarkable literary and epigraphic forgeries of the Renaissance (concerning the allegedly remarkable history of ancient Viterbo), Nanni obviously had the mind of prophecy (see Roberto Weiss, "An Unknown Epigraphic Tract by Annius of Viterbo," in *Italian Studies Presented to E. R. Vincent*, Cambridge, 1962, pp. 101–20, with a good bibliography, and "Traccia per una biografia di Annio da Viterbo," *Italia medioevale e umanistica*, V [1962], 425–41). Marino Sanudo, *Diarii*, VIII, ed. N. Barozzi, Venice, 1882, col. 326, relates the prophecies of a certain Fra Pietro Nanni, who was about ninety years old in May 1509: the Venetians had just suffered the disaster of Agnadello in the war of the League of Cambrai, and Pietro Nanni predicted that after losing all their dominion because of their sins, the Venetians would regain their territorial possessions (*tutto il suo stato*) after a "flagellation" of two and a half years. The year 1509 would be marked by famine and plague, but Venice would be spared. Nanni also said that "il Turcho si farà christian." The conversion of the Turk to Christianity was a favorite theme of prophecy.

Paolo Preto, *Venezia e i Turchi*, Florence, 1975, pp. 67–91, has dealt with various prophecies foretelling disaster for the Turks (and for Islam) from the later middle ages to the end of the seventeenth century, especially prophecies which involved Venice in her struggles with the Turk. It is easy to find such prophecies. For example, one Grani da Idra in a report of 24 November 1689 speaks of the unrest in Istanbul which was being increased by the discovery of an inscription written in Bulgarian letters on a slab of marble to the effect "che nell'anno 1691 doverà Constantinopoli cader in mano de'Christiani, e del 1693 serà tenuto un concilio per l'union delle chiese, e che ciò havesse aumentato fra Turchi la confusione!" (Arch. di Stato di Venezia, Provv. da terra e da mar, Filza 948, docs. unnumbered).

On the Turkish presence in Venice, especially in connection with the Fondaco dei Turchi on the Grand Canal from the sixteenth century to the eighteenth, see the interesting book of Bernard Lewis, *The Muslim Discovery of Europe*, New York and London, 1982, pp. 121–24.

to him by right, but also to establish in Naples and other south Italian ports the bases necessary for a crusade against the Ottoman empire.[21] Charles VIII dreamed of acquiring for himself the crown of the Palaeologi, and was depicted by contemporary artists decked out in Byzantine imperial accoutrements. He was probably influenced by a well-known prophecy current in his day that a French king named Charles would conquer Greece and subdue the Turk:

> Entrera puis dedans la Grèce,
> Où par sa vaillante prouesse
> Sera nommé le roy des Grectz.
> Et cecy fait, tantost après,
> Divinement sera escript
> Sur son front, qu'on lira, et dit:
> "Roy de France suis, des Rommains
> et des Grectz." Lors tous humains
> Subiuguera et Barbarins,
> Yspres, Turcs et aussi Surins. . . .[22]

For obvious reasons most Christian prophecies relating to the Turks foretold their ultimate doom, but from the accession of Sultan Murad II in 1421 the Turks had been marching constantly into victory. To be sure, their advance had been stopped at Belgrade, Rhodes, and Otranto, but Otranto was a beachhead into Italy. Before Christendom witnessed their final defeat, it was obvious that the Turks were going to win more victories, as certain astrological predictions made quite clear. Early in the year 1498, for example, the well-known

---

[21] Cf. Setton, *The Papacy and the Levant*, II (1978), chaps. 15–16, pp. 448ff.

[22] Guilloche de Bordeaux, *La Prophétie du roy Charles VIII*, ed. Marquis de La Grange, Paris: Académie des bibliophiles, 1869, p. 7; C. de Cherrier, *Histoire de Charles VIII*, I (2nd ed., Paris, 1870), 489; Börje Knös, *Un Ambassadeur de l'hellénisme, Janus Lascaris, et la tradition gréco-byzantine dans l'humanisme français*, Uppsala, 1945, p. 71. Barbarins are Berbères, inhabitants of Barbary; Yspres, Cyprus; and Surins, Syrians. On the various prophecies which preceded and attended Charles VIII's expedition and the *mystérieuse anxiété* which reigned in Italy early in 1494, see H.-F. Delaborde, *L'Expédition de Charles VIII en Italie*, Paris, 1888, pp. 313 ff.

Franciscan Thomas Murner addressed to the young Baron Hans Werner von Mörsperg a general prognostication for the year which lay ahead. The work was printed by Friedrich Riedrer in Freiburg im Breisgau (in 1498), and appears to exist in a single copy. It includes the following prediction: "The situation of the Turks depends upon Leo. Therefore everything, which they undertake this year, will prosper, especially in the summer, and the Church will suffer the greatest losses at their hands. Christians must be persuaded not to start anything with them in the summer, because they are bent upon acquiring renown." Murner's prediction also contains a grim warning to Pope Alexander VI *de statu suo miserando imminente.*[23]

The pontificate of Alexander VI gave rise to many warnings, most notably from Girolamo Savonarola, whose prophecies were largely concerned with the means God would employ to effect the needed reforms in the Church. Savonarola saw in Charles VIII God's chosen instrument of reform. The prophet's eyes were usually fastened upon Florence, and his purview did not often transcend the boundaries of Italy. Despite occasional references to the Turks, Savonarola was not much interested in Ottoman affairs. Most of what he knew of Islam probably came from a cursory reading of Peter the Venerable and Fra Ricoldo da Montecroce, who refuted Moslem doctrine as a debased heresy of Judaeo-Christian origin. That Islam was a fraudulent and inane superstition was a commonplace in western literature, and Savonarola, who had presumably never read the (Latin) Koran, had no doubt that it was all merely a compound of *fabulae ac mendacia*, lacking divine inspiration, rational bases, and intellectual content (*Mahumetanorum sectam omni ratione carere*).[24]

---

[23] *Practica anno domini MCCCCLXXXXVIII per fratrem Thomam Murner . . . compilata*, in Moriz Sondheim, *Thomas Murner als Astrolog*, Strassburg, 1938, pp. 58, 70, 80 (in the Schriften der Elsass-Lothringischen Wissenschaftlichen Gesellschaft zu Strassburg, Reihe A., vol. XX).

[24] Savonarola, *Commentatiuncula lectu dignissima*, in Th. Bibliander, *Machumetis Saracenorum principis eiusque successorum vitae, doctrina, ac ipse Alcoran* (ed. of March 1550), II [pp. 233–36], and cf. Aldobrandino Malvezzi, *L'Islamismo e la cultura europea*, Florence: Sansoni, 1956, pp. 123, 147.

In Florence the art of prophecy did not die with Savonarola. During the troubled years that followed Charles VIII's
expedition into Italy and Piero de' Medici's expulsion from
the city, prophetic assurances were sought of divine aid
against political uncertainty, social strife, ecclesiastical cor-
ruption, the Turkish menace, and other sources of current apprehension. Among those who searched the prophetic books
of the Bible for knowledge of the future was the Florentine
merchant Francesco da Meleto, who in the 1470's had been
in Constantinople, where he had discussed with Jews the
problem of their conversion. The date of Francesco's return
to the Arno is not known, but he was almost certainly a wit-
ness to the events of Savonarola's short but spectacular career
as virtual ruler of Florence.

Francesco's recondite studies throve as the Holy Spirit
fired the ardor of the student and assisted the calculations of
the merchant, for the time came when he could announce
that the year 1517 would mark the precise beginning of a new
era with the conversion of the Jews, which would thereafter
be followed by the end of Islam. Anxious to share his knowledge of coming events, Francesco published a vernacular
dialogue entitled *Convivio de' secreti della Scriptura Santa*
(about 1510?). The interest accorded this work was apparently sufficient, some four years later, to inspire Francesco with
the desire to acquaint the recently elected pope, the Florentine Leo X, with the results of his prophetic lucubrations. He
therefore wrote in Latin a second book, which he dedicated
to Leo, on the *Quadrivium temporum prophetatorum*,
which stressed the same fact as the earlier work—that the predestined time was at hand when, in 1517, the Jews would be
converted to Christianity.

By now Francesco's prophetic vision had become clearer,
for in the *Quadrivium* he could date the end of Islam to the
year 1536, which would be particularly welcome news as
Europe was learning of Sultan Selim I's conquest of the Persians (1514) and fearing a similar victory over the Mamluks
(which was to come in 1516–1517). But however this may be,
Francesco da Meleto, *senex et pauperculus*, had the honor of
presenting the *Quadrivium* in person to the pope, who was

already planning a holy league against the Turks, hoping to take advantage of the sultan's preoccupation with the affairs of Persia, Syria, and Egypt. Francesco spent three months in Rome, in lodgings provided by the pope's secretary Pietro Bembo, and the *Quadrivium* was printed with money supplied by Antonio Zeno, provost of the church of Volterra. But it was dangerous to possess the gift of prophecy so soon after Savonarola and to lay claim to revelations from the Holy Spirit, and although his prognostics had appeared innocuous and encouraging enough to print, they seemed to take on sinister meanings as they were repeated from the pulpits and entered the streets and shops of Florence. The atmosphere was tense in Italy, for there were many more prophets than Savonarola and Francesco da Meleto on the scene. In May 1516, for example, a certain Fra Bonaventura, who was alleged to have 20,000 followers, appeared in Rome: He declared the pope excommunicate, attacked the Roman Church, and predicted that the king of France would effect the conversion of the Turks.[25]

As the year 1517 began, excitement increased among the Florentines, for this was Francesco da Meleto's first prophetic year, but apparently the local Jews showed no marked inclination toward conversion. In January 1517 a provincial synod was held in Florence, presided over by the Cardinal Arch-

---

[25] On Fra Bonaventura, cf. Ludwig von Pastor, *History of the Popes*, V (repr. 1950), 224–25, and *Gesch. d. Päpste*, III, pt. 1 (repr. 1955), 201. In 1509 an alleged letter of the Empress Helena of Ethiopia to King Manuel of Portugal insisted that the time was at hand when the prediction of Christ and the Virgin Mary would come true, namely that a king of France would appear "qui aboliturus esset universum barbarorum et Maurorum genus, et hoc ipsum quidem nunc tempus est, quod Christus benedictae suae matri futurum promisit . . ." (O. Raynaldus, *Ann. eccl.*, ad ann. 1509, no. 33, vol. XX [1694], 71). In 1510 a preacher in Verona prophesied a series of events to come at different dates, including the death of a great prelate in Rome; a miracle of Our Lady; heavy and continuous rains; plague; "terrible signs in the air, i.e., horses with armed men, all on fire;" comets; a great shedding of blood in Tuscany; and, finally, sometime before 1516, the destruction of some city in Lombardy (Sanudo, *Diarii*, X, ed. G. Berchet, Venice, 1883, cols. 48–49). The unique feature of these prophecies is that the preacher in Verona apparently offered to undergo torture if his predictions proved untrue or to remain incarcerated until their fulfillment!

bishop Giulio de' Medici, later Pope Clement VII, which for-
bade the reading of Francesco's books and even the possession of them, which helps to explain their extreme rarity today. The synodal sentence of condemnation also prohibited
the preachers from enunciating from the pulpits (as some had
been doing) Francesco's *nuova, erronea e presuntuosa dot-
trina* under pain of excommunication and perpetual depri-
vation of the license to preach. Francesco was now required
to write another book, retracting his errors and asking par-
don for his temerity and presumption, and this within two
months. He made a solemn abjuration of his errors, doubtless
startled by the sudden turn of the wheel of fortune. The acts
of the synod of Florence were confirmed by papal bulls dated
1 and 17 March 1517, and published on 12 April. As time
proved Francesco's prophecies to be quite as erroneous as the
synod of Florence had pronounced them, his name was for-
gotten, and his works did not even appear in the first indices
of forbidden books.[26]

A prophecy, which was said to have been sent from
England to Venice in 1519 shortly after Charles V's election
as emperor, foretold his destruction of the Ottoman empire
as well as his conquest of most of Europe.[27] Champion of
the Church against the Lutherans, heir to the Hapsburg do-

---

[26] S. Bongi, "Francesco da Meleto, un profeta fiorentino a' tempi del
Machiavello," in *Archivio storico italiano*, 5th ser., III (Florence, 1889),
62–70; cf. Pastor, *Gesch. d. Päpste*, III-1, 199–200; André Chastel, "L'Anté-
christ à la Renaissance," in Enrico Castelli, ed., *Christianesimo e ragion
di stato: L'Umanesimo e il demoniaco nell'arte*, Rome and Milan, 1952,
pp. 177–86; Chastel, *Art et humanisme à Florence au temps de Laurent
le Magnifique*, Paris, 1961, pp. 343–46, 453–54; Eugenio Garin, "Paolo
Orlandini e il profeta Francesco da Meleto," in *La Cultura filosofica del
Rinascimento italiano*, Florence, 1961, pp. 213–23; and see especially
Cesare Vasoli, "La Profezia di Francesco da Meleto," in the *Archivio di
filosofia*, Padua, 1963, no. 3, pp. 27–80, with selected texts from Francesco da Meleto's *Convivio* and *Quadrivium*. See also Vasoli's article on
"L'Attesa della nuova era in ambienti e gruppi fiorentini del Quattrocento,"
in *L'Attesa dell'età nuova nella spiritualità della fine del medioevo*, Todi,
1962, pp. 370–432 (Centro di studi sulla spiritualità medievale, III).

[27] Sanudo, *Diarii*, XXVIII, 133, included in entries under December,
1519: ". . . transiens mare cum magno exercitu intrabit Graeciam et rex
Graecorum nominabitur, subiugans . . . Turchos. . . ."

minions in eastern Europe, Charles was inevitably cast in the role of crusader. Prophecy was bound to embellish his career. In 1534 the Viennese printer Johann Singriener (it was apparently he) brought out a work called *De eversione Europae prognosticon*, attributed to the Ferrarese physician and astrologer Antonio Torquato (properly Arquato), who had published five prognostics relating to the Aragonese house of Naples during the years 1491–1495. The *Prognosticon* of 1534 appeared without indication of place or printer. It was presumably inspired by the Turks' failure before Vienna in 1529 and their subsequent reverses in Syria and Austria in 1532. It was probably intended as propaganda for Charles V's crusade against Tunis in 1535. This prophecy of the Turks' ultimate defeat received wide currency in Europe from frequent re-editions in the sixteenth and seventeenth centuries, and was brought out in German, French, and even English translations.

The *Prognosticon* of Torquato (Arquato) was supposedly made to Matthias Corvinus, the king of Hungary, in 1480, a year made memorable by the Turkish occupation of Otranto and the first siege of Rhodes. It was represented as extending to the year 1538, by which time the Ottoman empire would have fallen (*antequam annus Domini 1538 finiatur*), owing to the sultan's defeat and death. According to the prophecy, however, the Turks would first make many conquests in the Levant. They would take Belgrade and Rhodes, and invade Hungary at a time when the country was torn by internecine strife. A king of Hungary would die fighting, and discord would complicate defense of the country as well as succession to the throne. The Turks would assail Hungary and Pannonia, as well as Apulia, Sicily, and the coasts of France and Spain, but they would finally fail in their attacks upon the Holy Roman Empire, exciting the "fury of the Germans, the vigor of the Hungarians, the armed might of the Spaniards, and the ingenuity of the Italians." There would be a great Spanish king on hand to oppose the Turks, "et forte ipse quoque aderit Caesar."

The Turkish sultan was destined to be killed, and his death would cause ruinous discord among his chief followers.

Greece would be laid waste by war, plague, and famine. The Venetians would succumb to Turkish assault. But Christ would at last reconcile the Christians; all Europe was going to respond in a vast crusade overseas. Victory would attend the crusaders' arms, and would effect the conversion of the Turks to Christianity. The Ottoman empire and the Holy Roman Empire would be united under a single emperor. The Moslems and Jews would receive Christian baptism.[28]

When the prophetic year 1538 had passed without divine intervention bringing about defeat of the Turks, a later edition of the *Prognosticon* (1552) states that the "house of Osman will fail under the thirteenth [i.e., before the year 1603], fourteenth [1617], or fifteenth ruler [1618], and will not exceed that number" *(Othomanni namque domus in XIII, XIIII, vel XV capite deficiet neque numerum excedet).* The prognostication attributed to Torquato occurs in various other anti-Turkish contexts which need not be explored here.[29] Such is the exactitude of its foreknowledge that even

---

[28] N. Iorga, *Notes et extraits*, V (1915), doc. no. XCIII, pp. 85–86, and Jean Deny, "Les Pseudo-Prophéties," *Revue des études islamiques*, X, 207–9. On Johann Singriener (Syngriener, Latin Singrenius), the outstanding printer of his time in Vienna (1510–1545), see Anton Mayer, *Wiens Buchdruckergeschichte*, I (Vienna, 1883), 37ff., and cf. Josef Benzing, *Die Buchdrucker des 16. und 17. Jahrhunderts im deutschen Sprachgebiet*, Wiesbaden, 1963, p. 455. Singriener's heirs continued his press after his death. Mayer seems not to list the *De eversione Europae prognosticon* among Singriener's productions. Michael Denis, *Wiens Buchdruckergeschichte bis MDLX*, Vienna, 1782, pp. 630–31, assigns it to Singriener, and cf. G. W. Panzer, *Annales typographici*, IX (repr. 1963), no. 362, p. 63. The British Library catalogue lists editions of 1535 and 1536, printed at Antwerp, "typis I. Graphaei" (*General Catalogue of Printed Books*, XXXIV [1941], col. 560, under Anselmus and Christophorus Cella, and cf. vol. 240 [1964], cols. 220–21, under Antonius Torquatus). The B. L. lists a German version of 1558 and Wm. Atwood, *Wonderful Predictions of . . . A. Torquatus*, London, 1689. There is a Spanish version of Torquato's complete prognostication in a MS. of about 1600 or later in the Bibl. Apost. Vaticana, Cod. lat. 7,750, fols. 300ʳ–303ʳ: "Pronóstico del maestro Antonio Torcato, natural de la ciudad de Ferrara, do[c]tor en artes y medicina y excelentisimo astrólogo, de la destrucción de toda Europa, el qual dirigió al serenisimo rey de Ungria Mathias, el año de 1480."

[29] Deny, "Les Pseudo-Prophéties," pp. 209–16, and on Antonio Arquato or Torquato, cf. Lynn Thorndike, *History of Magic and Experimental Science*, IV (1934), 467ff., 481, and vol. V (1941), 179.

a casual perusal of the text makes clear its spurious nature. From the same period in which it was so popular, however, there comes another and much more important prophecy which was interpreted in Europe as foretelling the final failure of the Turks, a *vaticinium infidelium lingua Turcica* [*scriptum*]. This prophecy was rightly believed to be of Turkish origin, and is preserved for us by a certain Bartholomaeus Georgievicz, one of the most widely read of all writers who published accounts of the Turks in the sixteenth century.

Bartholomaeus Georgievicz
and the "Red Apple"

Bartholomaeus Georgievicz (or Gjorgjević) has been identified as a Hungarian or Croatian noble, called B. Gywrgyewych de Mala Mláka, who on 16 March 1519 represented two Croatian nobles before the cathedral chapter of Agram (Zagreb), and who is mentioned on 28 October 1525 with his brothers as possessors of certain properties between the rivers Kupa and Una. On 25 November 1526, however, the brothers appear as owners of these properties without Bartholomaeus, who had been captured by the Turks after the battle of Mohács (at the end of August 1526). Still very young at this time, Bartholomaeus was to spend almost a decade as a slave in Istanbul, Thrace, and Asia Minor.[30]

Employed as a shepherd and cultivator of the soil, a groom and even a soldier of sorts, Georgievicz knew the hardships of sleeping beneath the open sky both in summer and in winter. On one occasion he escaped from servitude, lived for some time on nuts, fruits, and herbs, and with the guidance

---

[30] The best study of Georgievicz is by Franz Kidrič, "Bartholomaeus Gjorgjević: Biographische und bibliographische Zusammenfassung," in *Museion: Veröffentlichungen aus der Nationalbibliothek in Wien, Mitteilungen*, II (1920), 10–11, 25ff., where facts are given from the important article by V. Klaić, "Prilozi za životopis Bartola Georgijevića," *Vjesnik hrv.-slav.-dalm. zem arkiva*, XIII (Zagreb, 1911), 129–41. Kidrič also shows that Bartholomaeus Georgius Pannonius, who has left an autobiographical account of his Turkish captivity and various adventures (in Kidrič, *op. cit.*, pp. 12–18), is none other than Georgievicz. Of the identity of the two there can be no doubt. (Only 200 copies of Kidrič's monograph were printed.)

of the northern stars made his way to the Hellespont across the tracks of wild beasts. He tried to cross the strait on a hastily improvised raft, but was caught, returned to his owner, severely beaten in punishment for his daring, and turned over to slave dealers for resale to more vigilant masters. Adhering always to the Catholic faith, if we may believe his own account, Georgievicz was bought and sold seven times. Finding the shorter way home through Thrace too hazardous for another try, when he escaped again (for the fourth time!), he followed the southern stars through Caramania and the deserts of Syria to Damascus, where he taught Greek for some time, and later made his way into the Holy Land, where he was helped by the Franciscans of Mount Zion, with whom he spent about a year (1537). Thereafter he returned to Europe as a "herald of Turkish cruelty." He gives us the details of his life in an autobiographical sketch,[31] as well as in the various prefaces and dedicatory letters prefixed to his published works, which first began to appear in Antwerp in 1544, and soon "attained a phenomenal European popularity which continued through the seventeenth century."[32] Georgievicz died in Italy, probably in Rome, late in the year 1566.[33] In his own day he was almost as widely read as Luther. One most interesting aspect of Georgievicz's work is that it shows the Christians believed themselves to have no monopoly of prophecies relating to the ultimate destruction of the Ottoman empire. The Turks had such a prophecy, which Georgievicz first made known to Europe in 1544.

In addition to a rather lengthy book on the *Pellegrinaggio della Terra Santa*, Georgievicz published a number of much briefer works (more frequently reprinted) on Turkish rites and ceremonies, military affairs, agriculture, and the suffering of Christians under the Turkish regime, as well as a little Turkish-Latin phrasebook (also in the vernacular languages,

---

[31] Cf. Kidrič, "Bartholomaeus Gjorgjević," *Museion, Mitteilungen*, II (Vienna, 1920), 12–17.

[32] Clarence D. Rouillard, *The Turk in French History, Thought, and Literature (1520–1660)*, Paris, 1938, pp. 189–95, 272–73.

[33] Cf. Kidrič, *op. cit.*, pp. 27, 28.

but not seriously intended as a traveler's *parleur*), an exhortation against the Turks, and (among other short pieces) the "prophecy of the infidels in the Turkish language."[34] This prophecy, called in the Latin editions *Vaticinium Infidelium lingua Turcica*, Georgievicz gives both in transliterated Turkish and in translation, together with a detailed commentary on every phrase of the original. The translation of the text is of course much easier than the exegesis of its inner meaning:

> Our emperor [the sultan] will come, he will take away the kingdom of an unbelieving prince, and will also seize the Red Apple [Kuzul Almi] and hold it under his sway. If unto the seventh year the sword of the Christians shall not have arisen, unto the twelfth year shall he rule them. He will build houses, plant vineyards, put hedges around the gardens, and beget children [which may mean that the Grand Turk will construct mosques and public buildings, establish new colonies, conquer new cities and fortify them, and foster the spread of Islam everywhere in the Ottoman empire]. After the twelfth year, from the time the Red Apple shall have been made to submit to his power, the sword of the Christians will appear, which will turn the Turk around and put him to flight.[35]

---

[34] Rather confused and incomplete listings of Bartholomaeus Georgievicz's works are given in J. Ch. Brunet, *Manuel du libraire*, II (Berlin, 1922), cols. 1540–42, and J. G. Th. Graesse, *Trésor de livres rares et précieux*, III (Berlin, 1922), 53–54; cf. also R. Röhricht, *Bibliotheca geographica Palaestinae*, Berlin, 1890, pp. 189–90. The best bibliographical guide to Georgievicz's works is Kidrič, "Bartholomaeus Gjorgjević," pp. 19–24, where 82 different editions, reprints, translations, and adaptations of Georgievicz's works are listed from 1544 to 1686. Cf. also the philological study of A. R. Nykl, *Gonzalo de Argote y de Molina's "Discurso sobre la poesía castellana"* . . . *and Bartholomaeus Gjorgjević*, Baltimore, 1948, 28 pp. Carl Göllner, *Turcica: Die europäischen Türkendrucke des XVI. Jahrhunderts*, II (Bucharest and Baden-Baden, 1968), nos. 924, etc., 2444–45, pp. 30ff., 720–21, lists 23 Georgievicz imprints from 1552 to 1600.

[35] Bartholomaeus Georgievicz, *De Turcarum moribus epitome, Bartholomaeo Georgievicz Peregrino auctore*, Lyon: Ioan. Tornaesius, 1553, pp. 109–24, the Turkish text and Latin translation being given on pp. 109–10, J. Deny, "Les Pseudo-Prophéties," p. 218, gives a corrected, modernized version of the Turkish text, which may be also found (in the old Arabic script) in J. Mordtmann, "Türkisches," *Mittheilungen des Seminars für*

There were those who identified the "Red Apple" as Constantinople, or even Buda, but some exegetes took it to mean Rome. In the seventeenth century the Turkish traveler Evliya

---

Orientalische Sprachen . . . zu Berlin, V, pt. 2 (1902), 167–68. Tornaesius'
edition of 1555 is a reprint of that of 1553, with some resetting of type,
especially in the first portion of the book. The Gennadius Library in Athens
also has editions, "apud Ioan. Tornaesium," of Lyon, 1578; *sine loco*, 1598;
and of Geneva, 1629. (My notes suggest that from p. 14 all these Tornaesius
imprints have the same pagination.) Georgievicz's *Epitome* was published
more than a dozen times between 1553 and 1600, and retained its popularity throughout the seventeenth century.

    The earliest editions of Georgievicz that I have seen are the *De Tur-
carum ritu et caeremoniis*, Antwerp: "apud Gregorium Bontium," 1544,
with a dedicatory letter dated at Louvain on 1 January 1544 to the imperial
chamberlain Ludwig van Praet (*Lodovico de Praet*), and the *De afflictione
tam captivorum quam etiam sub Turcae tributo viventium Christianorum*, also Antwerp: "typis Copenii," 1544, with a dedicatory letter to the
Emperor Charles V dated at Louvain on 15 March.

    These two books, both in the Gennadeion, are apparently Georgievicz's
first appearance in print. The latter, *De afflictione*, has seven fine half-page
woodcuts illustrating Christian sufferings or misadventures at Turkish
hands, as well as a full-page woodcut portrait of Georgievicz on the reverse
of the last page, showing him dressed in a pilgrim's cloak, equipped with
a staff, offering a book to the crucified Christ, with the inscription,
Dirupisti domine vincula mea, tibi sacrificabo hostiam laudis. (Both the
De ritu et caeremoniis and *De afflictione* are given in the Tornaesius editions.) The same seven half-page woodcuts which appear in the Latin
version of the *De afflictione* (but not Georgievicz's portrait) are also reproduced in the French translation which appeared contemporaneously in
Antwerp, *Les Misères et tribulations que les Christiens tributaires et
esclaves tenuz par le Turcz seuffrent . . .*, "imprimé en Anvers par Jehan
de Grave," 1544, with the letter (here undated) to Charles V. This translation was apparently prepared from the Latin text. There is also a Flemish
edition of the *De afflictione*, as well as French and German editions of the
De ritu et caeremoniis, which I have not seen. On the French translations
and their re-editions, cf. C. D. Rouillard, *The Turk in French History*,
p. 189. The prophecy of the Red Apple may also be found in the collection
of Theodor Bibliander, *Machumetis Saracenorum principis eiusque successorum vitae, doctrina*, etc. (ed. of March 1550), *ad fin.*, pp. 166–69.

    Georgievicz's works were immensely popular; being brief and informa-
tive, they were easily read. They were often reprinted, as we have noted,
the Gennadeion having fifteen different editions, a number of them quite
unknown to Brunet and his fellow bibliographers. Some of them are most
interesting. The Gennadeion has, for example, a copy of the *Opera nova
che comprende quattro libretti* [containing the *Pellegrinaggio della Terra
Santa; Della Miseria così de i prigioni, come anco de Christiani, che
vivono sotto il tributo del Turco; Profetia de i Turchi, della loro rovina*;

Constantinople

Efendi says that more than a thousand years before his time there had been an image of the Virgin in S. Sophia,

holding in her hand a carbuncle as big as a pigeon's egg, by the blaze of which the mosque was lighted every night: this carbuncle was

---

and *Epistola essortatoria contra l'Infideli*], "in Roma appresso Antonio Barre," 1555, in the original brown calf binding, with a cardinal's arms and the inscription in gold on the upper cover: *Illustriss. principi et reverendissimo D[omino]*, and on the back cover: *Hippolito Card. Ferr., author D.D.*, showing the volume to be Georgievicz's presentation copy to Lucrezia Borgia's son, the well-known Hippolito d'Este (created a cardinal in December 1538, Hippolito died in 1572). Cf. L. A. Paton, *Selected Bindings from the Gennadius Library*, Am. Sch. Classical Studies, Athens, 1924, p. 23 and pl. XXI. This edition of the *Opera nova* was intended for sale "alla bottegha del segno della Gatta, in campo di Fiore."

Another edition of Georgievicz's works, in Latin, entitled *Libellus vere Christiana lectione dignus diversas res Turcharum brevi tradens*, "impressum Romae apud Anthonium Bladum impressorem cameralem XV. Septemb.," 1552, contains a dedicatory letter dated at Rome two days earlier (13 September) to Cardinal Innocenzo del Monte, who had been the sole recipient of a red hat in Julius III's first creation of cardinals (in May 1550). This edition was also to be sold "tribus iuliis exemplar apud Magistrum Ioannem in insignio Gattae in campo Floris;" the copy in the Gennadeion shows the Turkish prophecy to have been studied about the year 1600 or so by some previous owner who marked certain passages in red ink.

In 1554 Georgievicz presented to Nicolaus Olah, archbishop of Gran and primate of Hungary, a copy of his *Specchio della peregrinatione delli più notabili luoghi della Terra Santa di promessione, et delle processioni et cerimonie, che nella città di Hierusalem si sogliono celebrare*, Rome: "per Valerio Dorico," 1554, with the inscription (cf. that to Cardinal Hippolito d'Este), "Illustrissimo ac reverendissimo D., domino Nicolao Olaho, archiepiscopo Strigoniensi et regni Hungariae cancellario, D. et benemerito suo patrono, Author D. D., MDLIIII." From the number of "patrons" whom Georgievicz acknowledged in the publication of his books, he would seem to have been much dependent for a living upon the ἀντίδωρα he received for his dedicatory letters and presentation copies.

Georgievicz had also appeared in the Italian translation of Lodovico Domenichi in the *Prophetia de maometani, et altre cose Turchesche*, Florence, 1548, with a dedicatory letter dated "in Lovagno alli XVII di Marzo l'anno MDXLV" (unnum. fol. 6^r = Avi), addressed to Cardinal Otto Truchsess, bishop of Augsburg, to whom Paul III had given the red hat in his eighth creation of cardinals on 19 December 1544 (Otto Truchsess died in 1573). Part of Domenichi's translation was used in the *Opera nova*, referred to above. It was also appended to Giovanantonio Menavino, *Della Legge, religione et vita de'Turchi . . ., Oltre ciò, una prophetia de' Mahomettani, et altre cose Turchesche, non più vedute, tradotte da M. Lodovico Domenichi*, Venice ["appresso Vincenzo Valgrisi"], 1548. The copy of this

. . . removed in the birthnight of the Prophet to Kizil Almà (Rome), which received its name (Red Apple) from thence.''[36]

The Red Apple was even associated with the gilded dome of S. Peter's.[37] In this connection it must be noted that although Kizil Elma means Red Apple, and was usually so understood among both Greeks and Latins, it can also mean Golden Apple.[38] Hasluck sees some vague connection between the pomegranate, as a symbol of power and abundance, and the Red Apple; the Arabic word for pomegranate is *Rummam*, "which gives a distinct point if the 'Red Apple' means Rome."[39]

The Red Apple symbolized world dominion. Georgievicz notes that in some of their books the Turks had *Urum Papa-si* as well as *Kizil Elma [Almà]*, "Red Apple," *id est, rubrum*

---

work in the Gennadeion, in a handsome contemporary binding of Venetian calf with gold tooling, lacks the name of the printer and the date and place of imprint (Domenichi's translation of Georgievicz's Turkish prophecy, *De afflictione*, etc., occupies pp. 183–250). This work was republished, with slight changes in the text, as *I Costumi et la vita de' Turchi, di Gio. Antonio Menavino . . . Con una prophetia et altre cose Turchesche, tradotte per M. Lodovico Domenichi*, Florence: "appresso Lorenzo Torrentino," 1551. Menavino was born about 1490. Captured by a Turkish corsair when he was about twelve years old, he was brought up in the seraglio of Sultan Bayazid II, whom he served as a page, regaining his freedom in 1513. Menavino is the chief source for the story that after his deposition from the throne Bayazid was poisoned by order of his son and successor Selim I (Hammer, IV, 122–23; Fisher, *Foreign Relations of Turkey*, p. 111; Alderson, *Structure of the Ottoman Dynasty*, tab. XXVIII). Georgievicz's works comprise the bulk of a small volume called *De origine imperii Turcorum*, to which on 1 January 1560 Melanchthon wrote a preface: this volume, published in Wittenberg in 1560, without indication of the printer, was translated into English by Hugh Goughe (see, below, notes 51–53).

[36] Evliya Efendi, *Narrative of Travels in Europe, Asia, and Africa* [Evliya Čelibi, *Seyahatnamesi . . .*], trans. in part by Joseph von Hammer, 2 vols., London, 1846–50, I, 57, from Evliya's description of Constantinople and its environs in the 1630's.

[37] E. J. W. Gibb, *Hist. of Ottoman Poetry*, IV (London, 1905), 25, note 2.

[38] Franz Babinger, "Qizil Elma," *Der Islam*, XII (1922), 109–11, with various bibliographical data. *Kizil akçe* means "gold coins."

[39] F. W. Hasluck, *Christianity and Islam under the Sultans*, 2 vols., Oxford, 1929, II, 736–40, and cf. Hasluck's article "The Mosques of the Arabs in Constantinople," *The Annual of the British School at Athens*, XXII (1916–18), 171–74.

pomum, sive graecum sacerdotem vel patriarcham. Obviously *Urum Papa-si* might mean not only Greek priest or patriarch (ʿΡωμαίων πάπας), but also pope of Rome (ʿΡωμαίων πάπας).[40] Among the Turks Rome was easily and inevitably equated with the Red Apple.

Since the Turks had been in Constantinople for almost a century before Georgievicz's time, they could not fit the prophecy to their occupation of the Bosporus in 1453 (although this was presumably its original meaning).[41] But prophecies are almost immortal; once born, they refuse to die. When time and circumstance render them obsolete, they come to life again like the phoenix, with new plumage. For centuries Constantinople and Rome had been the two capitals of Christendom, and we know that, in the apocalyptic tradition of Islam, "la ville de Rome a pris la place que la tradition plus ancienne réservait à Constantinople."[42] Identifying the Red Apple with Rome, the Turks talked constantly of an invasion of Italy. In the summer of 1480 the Turks captured Otranto, and Peter Schott, a classical scholar and canon of Strasbourg, says in a letter dated at Bologna on 6 March 1481 that he had just been to Rome in order to see the city before its conceivable capture by the Turks (. . . *ut si*

---

[40] Cf. R. M. Dawkins, "The Red Apple," in ᾿Αρχεῖον τοῦ Θρακικοῦ Λαογραφικοῦ καὶ Γλωσσικοῦ Θησαυροῦ, VI, Suppl. [᾿Επιτύμβιον Χρήστου Τσούντα], Athens, 1941, pp. 401–6. In (modern) Greek legends to drive the Turks "to the Red Apple Tree" (στὴν Κόκκινη Μηλιά) means to force their retreat into Asia whence they had originally come (Dawkins, p. 403). However, cf. Deny, "Les Pseudo-Prophéties," p. 218. The text of Georgievicz may be found in the collection of Bibliander, *ad fin.*, p. 167.

[41] It is impossible to say how old the Turkish prophecy of the Red Apple was when Georgievicz first reported it to Europeans, and so I am not sure that Deny, "Les Pseudo-Prophéties," p. 219, is entirely correct in saying that "les Occidentaux se sont trompés en y voyant, à la suite de Georgiewicz, une allusion à la prise de Constantinople," since the Turks probably first identified the Red Apple with Constantinople (cf. the quotation from Evliya Efendi, above) and then, after they had taken the city in 1453, with Rome, the capture of which now became their major military ambition.

[42] A. Abel, "Un Hadit sur la prise de Rome dans la tradition eschatologique de l'Islam," *Arabica*, V (1958), 12, *et passim*. (Abel does not mention the prophecy of the Red Apple.)

a Thurcis sit capienda prius eam viderim).[43] Although the Turks soon lost their beachhead at Otranto, they frequently raided the Italian coasts.

Georgievicz understood that the Turks associated the Red Apple with Rome, but he also knew of the earlier interpretation of the prophecy in which Constantinople had been the objective. Since the original version obviously foretold the capture of Constantinople, *also called the New Rome*, it was bound to receive a welcome hearing in Europe. The final Christian triumph over Islam was not expected, even in western prophecies (as we have seen), until further Turkish successes and the eleventh-hour victory of some Christian monarch. The Christians must bravely resist and patiently abide the attacks of Suleiman the Magnificent. Their turn would come.

In the meantime the seers were, as usual, bent upon disaster. In a prophecy allegedly discovered in 1594 the Abbot Verdino of Otranto was warned by his guardian angel of certain dire events to come. Verdino kindly shared his knowledge of the future with his disciples Jacopo of Otranto and Mauro of Palermo. In his dismal vision, which involved strange natural phenomena, *unde omnia ruent in peius*, serpents would multiply almost without number; they would fill the chambers of clerics, and priestly dignities would be stained with a vast effusion of blood. Famine would sweep every corner of the earth. Cities would perish by internal as well as by external upheavals, especially in Italy. The Turks would again lay waste to Otranto; Rome would be shattered; Florence would be reduced in size; and Bologna, the home of learning, would be almost abandoned. Lombardy would be overwhelmed. Milan and Genoa would feel the enemy's heavy hand. Turkish ships would despoil Venice. The kingdom of Sicily was doomed. Monasteries would be destroyed. Much blood would flow in two battles to be fought by the

---

[43] Charles Schmidt, *Histoire littéraire de l'Alsace*, 2 vols., 1879, II, 10, note 22, cited by L. Thuasne, ed., *Diarium Johannis Burchardi Argentinensis*, III (Paris, 1885), pp. III–IV.

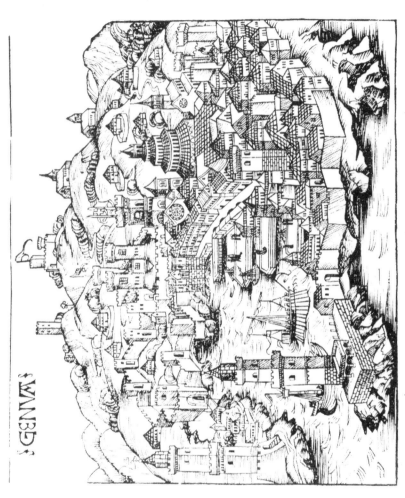

Genoa

French and Dutch. It was all quite terrifying. Would that God might avert his wrath![44]

Almost a century and a half after Georgievicz's report to Europeans of the Turkish prophecy of the Red Apple, which (he believed) foretold the eventual triumph of the Christian sword over the Ottoman empire and the expulsion of the Turk from the Balkans and from former Byzantine territory, the Sieur du Vignau, onetime secretary of a French ambassador to the Porte, made a similar report to Europe in his *État présent de la puissance ottomane* (Paris, 1687), which was dedicated to the grand duke of Tuscany, Cosimo III de' Medici, who was also the grand master of the crusading Order of S. Stefano. His book was immediately translated into English. Writing while Francesco Morosini was beginning his campaigns in Greece in the war which the Venetians had begun with the Porte in 1684,[45] during the reign of Sultan Mehmed IV (1649–1687), du Vignau says:

> And if this present expedition does not procure the entire ruin of the Turks, yet will it put their empire into such a great disorder, out of which they will never be able to raise themselves; and the arrogance of these infidels will be confounded, especially that of Vanli Effendi, preacher in ordinary to the Grand Seignior. This false prophet preaching in his Highness's hearing in the city of Caminiec two days after it was taken [in 1671], and congratulating him for this new conquest, foretold him with great assurance the conquest of Rome: seeing that according to some of their prophecies the Musselmen must take Spain and, in fine, predominate over the Red Apple; for thus do they call the city of Rome, *Kizil Alma*.

---

[44] Bibl. Apost. Vaticana, Cod. lat. 8,193, pars II (seventeenth century), fol 774; Cod. lat. 13,088 (eighteenth century), fols. 123^v–124^v; *I Futuri Destini degli stati e delle nazioni ovvero profezie . . .*, 5th ed., Turin, 1861, pp. 92–94. Most prophecies take a similar gloomy view of the future, like the *Vaticinii supposti di S. Cesareo, vescovo di Arles, ma però cavati da un libro intitolato "Liber mirabilis" stampato in lingua greca nel 1501, tradotto in latino* (Cod. Vat. lat. 9,415, pars II, fol. 299^v), on which cf. *Recueil complet des prophéties*, Lyon, 1870, p. 10; *I Futuri Destini*, p. 67; J. Ch. Brunet, *Manuel*, III (1882), 1741–42.

[45] Cf. K. M. Setton, *Venice, Austria, and the Turks in the Seventeenth Century*, Philadelphia, 1991, chaps. IX–XI, pp. 290ff.

He enlarged himself much on this matter, but took care not to fall in his discourse on another prophecy received by several of the most able persons amongst them, which says: They shall be driven from Rome, afterwards from Constantinople and the whole empire; that this which had been subdued and re-established by Constantine the Great was to be snatched from the Christians under the reign of another Constantine by a Turkish emperor named Mahomet; but that the Christians should also retake it during the reign of another Ottoman emperor of the same name.

It may be that this taking of the city of Rome, prophesied by the Turks, has been accomplished by Mahomet II in the same time he became master of Constantinople, where Constantine the Great, who was the restorer of it, and who gave it its name, having transferred the imperial seat from Rome, enacted it should be called New Rome. For being desirous to erect it as a capital of the Roman empire, he endeavored to equalize it to ancient Rome by the magnificence of its buildings, number of its inhabitants, and the rich spoils which he took from other cities of his obedience to make up the glory and splendor of this; and in consequence of this, the Grand Seigniors at this day call themselves *Roum Padichahi*, emperors of Rome, which is one of their finest titles. In fine, if the Christians have lost this capital of the eastern empire, which was also that of the Roman empire, under the reign of Constantine Paleologus, surnamed Dracosez; and if, for the accomplishment of the Turks' prophecy, he that took it was called Mahomet, the emperor who was so lately master of this famous city, and against whom the Christians have had such wonderful success, is also called Mahomet and consequently may well be he who according to the same prophecy shall restore it to the Christians. But if this explication be not sufficient, although it appears clear enough, may not one fancy after the manner of the eastern people that the Turks, being obliged to eat of the apple of discord and to make it red by the effusion of their own blood, shall see on themselves the accomplishment of their prophecy?[46]

---

[46] Le Sieur du Vignau, *L'État présent de la puissance ottomane, avec les causes de son accroissement et celles de sa décadence*, Paris, 1687, pp. 200–5; The Hague, 1688, pp. 156–60; *A New Account of the Present Condition of the Turkish Affairs, with the Causes of the Decay of the Otto-*

Although we cannot here embark upon a full study of the prophecies which foretold the destruction of the Ottoman empire in the sixteenth and seventeenth centuries, we may note that the legend of the Red Apple was the best known,

---

man Power, London, 1688, pp. 113–15. (The spelling and punctuation have been altered slightly.)

Vani Effendi made a considerable impression on seventeenth-century travellers to the Turkish capital, as shown in Thomas Smith's record of "a certain priest, one Vani Ephendi, famous for his eloquence, and who had gained a mighty opinion in the Court for his pretensions to extraordinary piety (consistent, by the practice and law of the Country, with a multitude of women, which he kept)" (*Remarks upon the Manners, Religion and Government of the Turks*, London, 1678, p. 172). Smith was a Fellow of Magdalen College, Oxford. On Vani Effendi, see also the account of his religious debate with Sir Thomas Baines, as recounted by the Rev. John Corvel, chaplain of the Levant Company in Istanbul from 1670 to 1679 (*Early Voyages and Travels in the Levant*, ed. J. T. Bent, Hakluyt Society, 1893, p. 271). On Vani Effendi, cf. also Setton, *Venice, Austria, and the Turks in the Seventeenth Century* (1991), 250–51.

Besides the prophetic literature mentioned elsewhere in this study, I have examined more than a dozen other contemporary works which explained to hopeful readers, in everything from long and learned monographs in Latin to four-page "letters" in the vernacular, the coming doom of Turkish power, of which I have especially noted the following: *La Declaratione delli horrendi segni apparsi in Constantinopoli et de uno insomnio fatto per il Gran Turcho, et con la pronosticatione de Barbarossa*, Milan: "per Vincentio da Medda," 1535, 8 pp., taking the form of a letter to an unidentified addressee; Pasqualino Regiselmo, *Vaticinia sive prophetiae Abbatis Ioachimi et Anselmi episcopi Marsicani*, Venice: "apud Ioannem Baptistam Bertonum," 1600, signatures H4^v–I1 and 01^v–02^v, on the Red Apple; *Monstres prodigieux advenus en la Turquie, depuis l'année de la comette, jusqu'en l'an présent 1624, menaçans la fin et entière ruyne de l'empire turquesque*, Paris: "chez Jean de Bordaeaux," 1624, 16 pp., relating to prodigies in Turkey from 1617 to 1624; *Copia d'una lettera venuta di Constantinopoli dove si narra i gran prodigii e spaventosi segni apparsi in detta Città e paesi circonvicini, con alcune horribili visioni apparse al Gran Turco . . .*, Messina, Naples and Florence: "per il Ciotti," 1630, 4 pp. (rather similar to *La Declaratione* of 1535), reprinted in a slightly abridged form in Milan as a *Nuova Rellatione o'vera copia d'una lettera*, with no date, and occurring also in a German version as a *Warhafftige Copia eines Schreibens aus Constantinopel*, etc., Hamburg, 1642, 8 pp., solemnly dated 1 September, 1641 (!), and ending with two brief selections from Luther's *Tischreden* referring to the prophecy of Daniel and the Turks; the erudite nonsense of Paul Pater, *Insignia Turcica, ex variis superstitionum tenebris, . . . nunc primum in lucem protracta*, Jena, [1685?], the date being inferred from the reference on p. 81 to "praesens annus MDCXXCV;" Niccolò Arnú, *Presagio dell'immi-*

and several works attest to its wide circulation.[47] These
prophecies are often accompanied by illustrations. The Turk
is sometimes shown, for example, rather precariously stand-
ing on what appear to be two cannon balls, holding in his extended left hand a flaming red apple, as in Artus Thomas

---

*nente rovina e caduta dell' impero ottomano, delle future vittorie e pros-
peri successi della Christianità*, Venice: "presso Pietro Antonio Brigonci,"
1686, who begins with the Turkish prophecy of the Red Apple (pp. 4–9),
which he identifies with Poland and the city of Caminietz [Kamenets—
Podolski, onetime capital of Podolia], the twelve years of the prophecy being the lapse of time between the Turks' occupation of Caminietz (1671)
and their great defeat at Vienna (1683); and *Nuova e vera Profezia di
Costantinopoli cadente . . .*, Venice: "per Sebastian Menegati," 1690. For
a few additional items, note Deny, "Pseudo-Prophéties," *Revue des études
islamiques*, X (1936), 205–7, and see in general Alphonse Dupront, "Croisades et eschatologie," *Archivio di filosofia*, 1960, nos. 2–3, pp. 175–98.

Prophecies of the coming destruction of the Ottoman empire were espe-
cially common in the seventeenth century. To the printed texts given above,
I would add the following notice which I found in the Arch. Segr. Vaticano,
Miscellanea, Arm. VI, tom. 39, fol. 120:

Regni Turcici Catastrophe Francisci Buderii Samogitiensis Philosophi celeberrimi
atque clarissimi Astrologi anno Christi 1244 exarata: Turcica gens ad totius orbis
imperium adspirans in Germaniam arma movebit anno salutari 1683 multa in-
ferendo damna Viennensibus atque Ungaris rebellantibus et fidem frangentibus
principi suo: sed Christus Christiani imperii subiugatam non ferens, Germanos
principes uno tantum ob sui defensionem deficiente et Polonie regem adducet
contra eos, nec civitas illa, que semper virgo erit obdormiet, dum omnipotens
Deus ex quodam suo fortalitio quatuor mille milites et postea duos elabi facit,
qui omnes ad pugnam confugient. Tandem magna strage circa medium Septem-
bris mensem Turcarum exercitus facta, ante eiusdem mensis elapsum magnus
armorum ductor a solo Polonie rege capietur atque interficietur. In quo prelio,
ut astra predicunt ob dicti regis ingenium, ductumque atque industriam Christianorum omnium maximus et sanctissimus princeps mortem immanissimi im-
peratoris Othomanorum una cum sui desolatione imperii videbit. Nam Otho-
manna domus nobis ita indicante magna cum Saturno Iovis coniunctione
corruet. Sic desinit Othomana potentia nam inter duos fratres, regnantem unum,
privatam de gente vitam alteram, bella intestina orientur, et dum curabunt unus
et alter se a tam magno pervastoque dominio expellere a foederatorum armis ab
illo expellentur ac denuo sancte crucis vexillum in orientem, tunc convolatum
videbimus.

For various other data also referring to events of the years 1683–1684, see
MS. cit., fols. 284ff.

[47] *Vaticinium Severi et Leonis Imperatorum, in quo videtur finis Turcarum in praesenti eorum Imperatore*, Brescia: "appresso Pietro Maria
Marchetti," 1596, pp. 79–95: "Habent Mauometani multa vaticinia, sed
nullum est apud ipsos tam celebre quam istud in quo continentur innu-
merabiles adversus Christianos victoriae, et tandem ipsorum excidium . . ."
(p. 79).

d'Embry's *Tableaux prophétiques prédisant la ruine de la monarchie turque* (1620)[48] and in Pietro Paolo Tozzi's *Profetie dell' Abbate Gioachino et di Anselmo, vescovo di Marsico* (Padua, 1625).[49] It should be observed of the latter work that the Turkish prophecy of the Red Apple is appended to the prophecies of Joachim and Anselm, but its (Turkish) text is not of course attributed to either of them. In Tobias Wagner's popular *Türcken-Büchlein* of 1664 the legend of the *rother Apffel* is fully recounted, and Georgievicz is given full credit as the source.[50] A year before this (in 1663) Michael Wendt had brought out in Wittenberg a special edition of *Doctor Martin Luthers Erschreckliche Türcken Propheceyung*, reprinting from the *Heerpredigt* Luther's exposition of the seventh chapter of Daniel as well as his admonitions "from the other part" of the same work, to which Wendt added a brief anthology of Luther's Turkish pronouncements drawn from his biblical commentaries, *Tischreden*, and other sources. Europe had been fed for generations on prophecies relating to the Turks. It was no wonder, for as Melanchthon wrote in 1560 in the preface to a work *De origine imperii Turcorum* (but consisting largely of Georgievicz's works), "We behold the Turkish power being extended over the human race while the kings and other princes of Europe dissipate their strength in domestic warfare. In the meantime the

---

[48] Artus Thomas d'Embry, *Tableaux prophétiques prédisant la ruine de la monarchie turque, et le rétablissement de l'empire grec*, "ouvrage imprimé en 1620," Lyon and Paris, repr. 1821, pp. 40–42 and fig. 17. The earliest edition of this work that I have seen is that appended to the second volume of Blaise de Vigenère's translation of Laonicus Chalcocondylas (2 vols., Paris, Cramoisy, 1650): *Tableaux prophétiques des empereurs Sévère et Léon, avec leurs epigrammes prédisans la ruine de la Monarchie des Turcs* (vol. II, fig. 17, p. 111). For earlier editions, cf. Graesse, *Trésor de livres rares et précieux*, II (1922), 111.

[49] Pietro Paolo Tozzi, *Profetie dell' Abbate Gioachino et di Anselmo, vescovo di Marsico, con l'imagini in dissegno . . . et un' Oracolo Turchesco*, Padua, 1625, pp. 77–78. The prophecies of the Abbot Joachim and Bishop Anselm had already been published by Pasqualino Regiselmo (Venice, 1589).

[50] Tobias Wagner, *Türcken-Büchlein: Summarische Beschreibung dess Ottomannisches Hauses Herkommen und Kriegen biss auff gegenwärtige Zeiten*, 1664, pp. 30–32.

Turks move onward. Eighty years ago [Johann] Hilten predicted that by the year 1600 the Turks would be ruling in Italy and Germany."[51] Shortly after Melanchthon had sponsored the publication of the *De origine imperii Turcorum*, it was translated into English by one Hugh Goughe, and "imprinted at London in Fletestreate, neare unto saint Dunstones church by Thomas Marshe," thus making the works of Georgievicz more easily available to English readers.[52] Obviously inspired by the preface of Melanchthon, whom he does not mention, Goughe declares in a dedicatory letter to Sir Thomas Gressam [Gresham] that

> . . . to the great damage and utter decay almost of Christes' infallible religion, the great Turkes' power and empire hath spredde itselfe so farre that at this instant ar[e] subiecte to his cruell tyrannye above foure and thirtye moste famous nations

[51] *De origine imperii Turcorum . . . Cui libellus de Turcorum moribus, collectus a Bartholemaeo Georgieviz, adiectus est, cum praefatione reverendi viri D. Philippi Melanchthonis*, Wittenburg, 1560. No printer is indicated. From sign. C8 the book consists of Georgievicz's *De Turcorum moribus epitome*, etc., and his works comprise about seven eighths of the total contents of the volume. Melanchthon's preface is dated 1 January 1560. Preceding Georgievicz's works are twelve brief biographies of the sultans from Othman to Suleiman, who "iam vero mortuus esse dicitur" (in 1560!), together with a list of the chief officers, judges, troops, and servitors of the Porte.

On 18 May 1552 Melanchthon wrote Johannes Matthesius that the Franciscan friar Johann Hilten of Eisenach had predicted that in 1516 papal power would begin to decline, and that by 1600 the Turks would rule in Italy and Germany (*Corpus reformatorum*, ed. C. G. Bretschneider, VII [Halle, 1840], cols. 1006–7): ". . . Iohannes Hilten Franciscanus . . . vaticinatus est anno MDXVI initium fore inclinationis pontificiae potentiae, . . . nec futuram esse restitutionem pontificiae au[c]toritatis. Idem praedixit Turcos in Italia et Germania regnaturos esse circiter annum MDC."

[52] *The offspring of the house of Ottomano, and officers pertaining to the greate Turkes Court, Whereunto is added Bartholomeus Georgieviz' Epitome of the custumes, rytes, ceremonies, and religion of the Turkes, with the miserable affliction of those Christians which live under their captivitie and bondage*, London: Thos. Marshe, about 1562–1563. Like his Latin original (1560), Goughe speaks of Sultan Suleiman, "whiche raigned in our time, but now is sayde to be dead" (unnum. fols. 12^v–13^r [= Biiii–v]). There were constant rumors in the West of sultans' deaths, but this line may show that Goughe wrote before Suleiman's death in 1566, or he would have altered the text as he sometimes did (note the reference to "English letters" on sign. $Iiiii^v$).

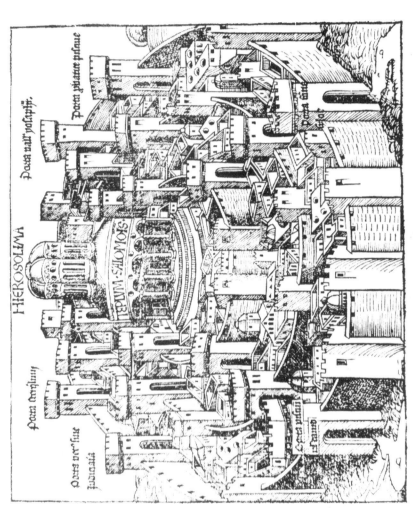

Jerusalem

whiche in times paste have bene christened, yea and within these fourescore years, as one Hiltenius by prophesyinge hathe foretolde us, he shall have dominion both in Italie and Germanie: ponderinge with myselfe this pitifull estate and lamentable ruyne of Christianitye, I imagined that it did not so become me, as by dutie I was bounde, . . . to reveale and make manifeste unto my countreymen the nature, disposition, customes, rites, and faithe of those circumcised infidelles, with the horrible rackinge, painefull tormenting, and unnaturall abusing of our faithefull bretheren, the innocent Christians most miserably oppressed with the heavye youke of their unmeasurable taxes, tributes, and continuall bondage. . . .[53]

In England as elsewhere thoughts of the Turk were accompanied by popular notions of lust and treachery, but mostly of stalwart performance in war. Various inns in Elizabethan England were known by the sign of the Saracen's Head: "When our Countrymen come home from fighting against the Saracens and were beaten by them," says John Selden, "they pictur'd them with huge bigg terrible faces (as you still see the Signe of the Saracen's head is) when in truth they were like other men, but this they did to save their owne creditts."[54] A Turk's head was employed as an archery butt, and one might practice by "shooting at the Turke." Even in faraway England the Turkish defeats at Malta in 1565 and at Lepanto in 1571 had brought a great relief, and, as Chew states, "prophecies of the overthrow of the Turks were naturally popular."[55] Although the Turkish defeats at Malta and Lepanto were, to be sure, a solace to the popular mind in

---

[53] Goughe, *The offspring of the house of Ottomano*, unnum. fol. 4 (= Aiiii). (I have modified the spelling slightly and the punctuation considerably.) On the extraordinary career of the great statesman, financier, and merchant, Sir Thomas Gresham, see Wentworth Francis Wentworth-Shields, in the *Dictionary of National Biography (DNB)*, VIII (repr. 1937–38), 585–96, where I note to my surprise that "Hugh Goughe dedicated to him, about 1570, his 'Ofspring of the House of Ottomano.'" Indeed, Wentworth-Shields missed nothing.

[54] John Selden (d. 1654), *Table Talk* (first published in 1689), ed. Sir Frederick Pollock, p. 136, cited by Samuel C. Chew, *The Crescent and the Rose*, New York, 1937, p. 146. On Selden, see Edward Fry, in the *DNB*, XVII, 1150–1162.

[55] Chew, *The Crescent and the Rose*, pp. 123–33, 140, 147.

England, they meant far more to the Spanish, the Italians, and the Austrians, to whom the Turks were a far greater threat than to the English. In Istanbul, however, there was now a rise of anti-Christian, especially anti-Catholic (and anti-Spanish) feeling, which played into the hands of the Protestants and, as time passed, proved of no small commercial advantage to England and Holland, where the upper bourgeois could easily moderate their hostility to Islam.

A remarkably large and interesting travel literature has come down to us from the sixteenth and of course the seventeenth century, bespeaking the hardihood of the many Europeans who ventured into the faraway domains of the Ottoman sultans, or who like Georgievicz were captured and escaped after years of servitude. Besides the tall tales which these wayfarers reported of their travels, much accurate information and many realistic appraisals of the Turks were also published. Georgievicz's works, for example, show a broad and genuine knowledge of Turkish life and manners. While he gives his readers a good deal of information concerning the religious practices of the Turkish Moslems, we need not believe that a certain class of dervishes (*monachi Dervislar vocati*) wore three-pound rings in their membra as guarantees of chastity.[56]

Thousands of fascinated readers learned from Georgievicz about the Turks' educational system and poetry, marriage and divorce, the pilgrimage to Mecca and Medina, the absurdities of the Koran, funeral ceremonies, military organization, provincial government, their unpretentious houses and rich apparel, the slave markets, Christian captives at work in the fields and pastures, the hardships of such a life, and the perils of flight. Georgievicz is much taken with Turkish cooking, especially with the bread baked with sesame seeds. The Turks had no taverns or public inns, such as Europeans were accustomed to, but vendors sold various kinds of food and

---

[56] Georgievicz, *De Turcarum moribus epitome*, Lyon, 1553, pp. 22–23: "Aliud genus [monachorum Turcorum] vidi qui incedunt pertusa verpa sive mentula, et incluso anulo aereo ponderis trium librarum a coitu disclusi ob servandam castitatem."

other necessities in the streets.[57] They sat on mats and tapes-tries to eat, cross-legged like tailors (*more sartorum*), their table being called a *tsophra*, made of leather apparently drawn on a frame. Giving a brief dialogue in Turkish with an interlinear translation, Georgievicz says, "I have added these few words of the Turkish language not for your use, gentle reader, but for your entertainment, so you may know how gross and barbarous they are: may the Almighty grant that they have more need of our language than we of theirs!" The dialogue itself is a lesson in distrust of the Turk. A Christian merchant, travelling alone, is urged by a Turk whom he meets to come home with him. The Turk has a big house, "like a castle," and very nearby: "Climb up and stand here . . . you'll see it over to the right. . . . Whom are you afraid of? Why won't you come?" But the Christian happens to be going in the opposite direction.[58]

All Christian subjects of the Porte paid a fourth of their in-comes in taxes, both those who labored in the fields and pas-tures and those who worked as handicraftsmen in the city shops. A capitation tax also fell on all Christian families, a ducat a head, and if parents could not pay, they were com-pelled to sell their children into servitude, and Turkish of-ficers were always collecting the most promising boys from Christian families (in the *devširme*), to forsake their religion and be lost to their families forever. A woodcut in Georgi-evicz's *De afflictione Christianorum* illustrates the Turkish seizure of children from their stunned parents.[59]

The printed book was the basis of learning and education in the sixteenth century. The popularity of Georgievicz's works is made evident by the large number of editions in

---

[57] Georgievicz, *Epitome* (1553), 64: "Nullae ibi tabernae hospitiis designatae aut publica diversoria, quemadmodum apud nostrates, tamen in plateis diversa venduntur cibaria et alia huiusmodi ad victum necessaria."

[58] Georgievicz, *Epitome* (1553), 68–73, and cf. *De Turcarum ritu et caeremoniis*, Antwerp, 1544, unnum fols. 21^r-22^r (=Fi-2).

[59] Georgievicz, *De afflictione tam captivorum quam etiam sub Turcae tributo viventium Christianorum*, Antwerp, 1544, unnum. fol. 11^r (=C3); reproduced also in the French translation of this work, *Les Misères et tribulations que les Christiens tributaires et esclaves tenuz par le Turcz seuffrent*, Antwerp, 1544, unnum. fol. 14^v (=Dii).

which they appeared. Crusaders and travellers had extended the European's geographical knowledge eastward generations before the Atlantic explorers had extended the *imago mundi* westward to include the New World. Travel has always excited as well as broadened the human mind. Homer and Dante fascinated their readers by taking them into the nebulous world beyond the grave. Modern astronomy acquired meaning for most people only when astronauts travelled into outer space. In the sixteenth century it was the Turks who most interested the Europeans. Before 1610, for example, twice as many French books were printed about Turkey as about North and South America; the titles relating to Turkey were reprinted more than four times as often as those concerning the Americas;[60] and in European libraries of the present time there are probably ten times as many brochures from the period before 1610 relating to the Turks as to events in the Americas.[61]

Although more than one writer of the sixteenth century asserted that possession of the art of printing showed in itself the superiority of European Christians over Turks and other infidels, there were also expressions of admiration for Turkish justice, military discipline, and government. The Turks were, to be sure, commonly regarded as *beaucoup pis que chiens*, but abuse lessened as knowledge increased, and we are informed by J. A. de Savigny in the *Discours sur les choses turques* (Lyon, 1606), attributed to Georgievicz, that the Turks left their vices at home while Christians took theirs into war. The Turks excluded pleasures from the camp, but the Christians welcomed every luxury and fancy food, and sometimes had more whores than soldiers in the army.[62]

---

[60] Geoffroy Atkinson, *Les Nouveaux Horizons de la Renaissance française*, Paris: Droz, 1935, pp. 10–12.

[61] Cf. Atkinson, *op. cit.*, p. 250.

[62] Atkinson, *op. cit.*, pp. 57, 177–79, 184–85, 211–12, 367–68, 397–99, and for sixteenth-century views of Turkish honor, charity, tolerance, etc., cf., *ibid.*, pp. 212–20, 240ff., 371–72, 385–86, 389ff.

Translations of the Koran and Increasing Tolerance of Islam

An objective knowledge of Islam, and therefore dispassionate judgments concerning the Turks, had been rather slow in coming. In the sixteenth and seventeenth centuries the process was much aided by the printing press. The far ends of the Christian world, Byzantium and Spain, had known Islam the best in earlier times, and had had the greatest cause to fear it. Much of what the Christians, especially eastern Christians, knew of Mohammed and Islam had come from the sparse notices to be found in the Byzantine sources, especially the *Chronographia* (to 813) of the early ninth-century monk Theophanes and its Latin translation by the papal librarian Anastasius (873–875); the chronicle, also of the ninth century, of George Hamartolus, and a polemic against Islam by one Bartholomaeus, a monk of Edessa, whose date remains uncertain; the later eleventh-century chronicle of John Skylitzes and its adaptation by George Cedrenus; and finally the *Panoplia dogmatica* of Euthymius Zigabenus (fl. 1100), a monk in the Constantinopolitan monastery of the Peribleptos.[63] Skylitzes-Cedrenus was apparently little known in the West.

---

[63] On the "puerile tales" of the Byzantines concerning Mohammed and Islam, cf. Aldobrandino Malvezzi, *L'Islamismo e la cultura europea*, Florence, 1956, pp. 62–72, readable but too brief. S. John Damascenus, who presumably knew Islamic doctrine well, has relatively little to say on the subject. The first Latin translation of Damascenus's major work does not come until about 1148–1150 when Burgundio of Pisa brought out his version of the *De fide orthodoxa* (cf. K. M. Setton, "The Byzantine Back-

The criticisms of Islam attributed to the Arab Christian al-Kindī, who (if he is the author of the *Risālah* or *Apology* in question) wrote about the year 830 at the court of the Caliph al-Ma'mūn, were also unknown in the West before the mid-twelfth century, when the *Apology* was translated from Arabic into Latin by Peter of Toledo at the behest of Abbot Peter of Cluny, who went to Spain in 1141–1142 on a general visitation of the Benedictine monasteries in the domains of Alfonso VII of León and Castile.[64]

During his sojourn in Spain Peter the Venerable found the English astronomer and geometrician Robert of Ketton and the latter's friend Hermann Dalmata in the Ebro valley. Both were accomplished Arabists; Spain was the center of Arabic studies in the West. At great expense Peter induced the two friends to prepare certain translations for him, of which Robert of Ketton's translation or rather paraphrase of the Koran was the most important. Hermann translated two texts to which were given the Latin titles *De generatione Mahumet* and *Doctrina Mahumet*. These works together with several others, including most notably Peter of Toledo's translation of the Pseudo-al-Kindī and Peter the Venerable's own *Liber contra sectam sive haeresim Saracenorum*, have now become known as the Cluniac Corpus or the Toledan-Cluniac Collection, which Mlle. M.-Th. d'Alverny has studied with brilliant effect.[65] This collection is particularly important,

---

ground to the Italian Renaissance," *Proceedings of the American Philosophical Society,* vol. 100 [1956], 24). See, further, Monneret de Villard, *Lo Studio dell' Islām in Europa nel XII e nel XIII secolo* (1944), esp. pp. 19–20, and cf. also K. Güterbock, *Der Islam im Lichte der byzantinischen Polemik*, Berlin, 1912, and W. Eichner, "Die Nachrichten über den Islam bei den Byzantinern," *Der Islam*, XXIII (1936), 133–62, 197–244.

[64] Cf. Wm. Muir, trans., *The Apology of Al-Kindy*, London, 1882; N. Daniel, *Islam and the West*, Edinburgh, 1960, *passim;* James Kritzeck, *Peter the Venerable and Islam*, Princeton, 1964, pp. 101–7.

[65] M.-Th. d'Alverny, "Deux Traductions latines du Coran au moyen-âge," *Archives d'histoire doctrinale et littéraire du moyen-âge*, XVI (Années XXII–XXIII, Paris, 1947–48), 69–98. The so-called *Doctrina Mahumet* is actually a dialogue of Mohammed with the Jew Abdia. The *Risālah* or *Apology* of the Pseudo-al-Kindī is earlier than the historian al-Bīrūnī (973–1028), who cites a passage from it (d'Alverny, *op. cit.,* p. 88). For the

Achaea

for it was often recopied (sometimes without the Pseudo-al-Kindī, of which extensive extracts were available in Vincent of Beauvais's *Speculum*), and was employed by various later Christian apologists against Islam such as (for the most famous example) Nicholas of Cusa, who saw a copy of the Cluniac Corpus in the Dominican convent at Pera in the course of his mission to Constantinople in 1437. Robert of Ketton's translation of the Koran, finished in the early summer of 1143, was not published until January 1543, when Theodor Bibliander (Buchmann) produced at Basel the famous volume *Machumetis Saracenorum principis eiusque successorum vitae ac doctrina, ipseque Alcoran. . . .*[66] Four years later (in 1547) Andrea Arrivabene published in Venice his Italian translation of the Koran, and although he claimed to have worked from the Arabic text, he had merely put into Italian Robert of Ketton's Latin version, which Bibliander had just published together with most of the texts in the Cluniac Corpus.[67] But Bibliander's edition had been issued

---

full contents of the Cluniac Corpus, see d'Alverny, *passim*, and for the MSS., *ibid.*, pp. 108–13, and Daniel, *Islam and the West*, pp. 399–400. On Robert of Ketton, see Thomas A. Archer, in the *DNB*, XVI, 1248–50.

[66] Cf. d'Alverny, "Deux Traductions," pp. 86, 103–5. The first edition of the Latin Koran was printed by the classicist Johannes Oporin of Basel, who had set up a press in 1541 with Thomas Platter. A letter of Sebastian Münster to his friend Konrad Pellikan, dated at Basel on 29 July 1542, refers to the difficulties in which Oporin became involved, owing to his dangerous enterprise in printing the Koran: ". . . De novis ista accipe: Oporinus periclitatur propter Alchoranum a se impressum. Nam hic liber ab universitate damnatus est isto tempore. Exspectatur magistratus sententia. Nec dubium, si evulgatus fuerit, damnabitur et ab imperatore . . ." (Karl Heinz Burmeister, *Briefe Sebastian Münsters*, Frankfurt am Main, 1964, p. 53).

[67] I have used Bibliander in the edition of 1550, which has a slightly different title (and pagination) from that of the first edition. See in general Monneret de Villard, *Lo Studio dell' Islām*, pp. 8–16; d'Alverny, "Deux Traductions," pp. 69–131; James Kritzeck, *Peter the Venerable and Islam*, esp. pp. 24ff., 62–65, 97–100. A second Latin translation of the Koran was made about 1210 by the Mozarab Mark, a canon of Toledo, at the behest of Archbishop Rodrigo Jiménez de Rada (d'Alverny, "Deux Traductions," pp. 113ff.). Mark of Toledo also translated a theological compendium known as the ʿAqīda, which he called in Latin the *Tractatus Habentometi* [i.e., Ibn-Tūmart!] *de unione Dei*, written by Ibn-Tūmart, the Mahdī of the Muwaḥḥids (Almohads) in the first half of the twelfth century, on which see the learned study by M.-Th. d'Alverny and Georges Vajda, "Marc de

cum scholiis et impiis annotationibus . . ., and was soon put on the Index,[68] for while the Curia Romana was always prepared to accept refutations of the Koran, it had little desire (at least in the mid-sixteenth century) to encourage objective studies of Islam. Refutations of the Koran were useful adjuncts to crusading propaganda.[69]

Tolerance was hardly to be expected of an age that still reviled the name of Epicurus and hated even the distant memory of Marcion and Pelagius. While hardly pro-Moslem, the strange but learned Guillaume Postel attempted an objective portrayal of Islam in his *République des Turcs*, first published at Poitiers in 1560. Postel tried to show that Protestants, Jews, and Moslems held many beliefs in common, for which (among other reasons) he earned the almost universal reprobation of his contemporaries.[70] But the wars of reli-

---

Tolède, traducteur d'Ibn Tūmart," in *Al-Andalus*, XVI (Madrid, 1951), 99–140, 259ff., and, *ibid.*, XVII (1952), 1ff. Monneret de Villard, *Lo Studio dell' Islām*, pp. 21–24, has confused the date of Mark of Toledo's translation of the Koran (1210) with his translation of Ibn-Tūmart (1213). Cf. d'Alverny, "Deux Traductions," p. 123 and note 3.

Although Mark of Toledo's Koran adheres much more closely to the Arabic text than that of Robert of Ketton, it had very little circulation. The great prestige of Peter the Venerable, however, helped secure a wide currency for Robert of Ketton's translation, which (as we have noted) was the one reprinted by Bibliander in his editions of 1543 and 1550.

[68] Monneret de Villard, *Lo Studio dell' Islām*, pp. 31–32, note 3.

[69] The first edition of the Koran is said to have been printed at Venice before 1518 by Paganino de' Paganini, but no bibliographer has seen this edition which, it has been suggested, was destroyed by papal requirement (F. J. Norton, *Italian Printers, 1501–1520*, London, 1958, pp. 116–17). There seems to be no evidence of the papal suppression of this edition, however, which does not appear in the *Indices librorum prohibitorum* (Monneret de Villard, *Lo Studio dell' Islām*, pp. 31–32, note 3). Chew, *The Crescent and the Rose*, p. 434, note 2, gives no evidence for the statement that "the *Koran* in Arabic was first printed at Venice between 1485 and 1499."

[70] Geoffroy Atkinson, *Les Nouveaux Horizons de la Renaissance française*, pp. 22–23, 227, 245–49; C. D. Rouillard, *The Turk in French History* (1938), pp. 206–12, 290–91, 321–22, 335–37, *et alibi*; Wm. J. Bouwsma, *Concordia Mundi: The Career and Thought of Guillaume Postel (1510–1581)*, Cambridge, Mass., 1957, pp. 202–5, 245, 262, 269–71. On Postel's prophetic expectations and the intricacies of his thought, see especially François Secret, "Guillaume Postel et les courants prophétiques de la Renaissance," *Studi Francesi*, 1957, no. 3, pp. 375–95, with a passing ref-

gion were exhausting, whether fought with the sword or the pen, and time brought at least some measure of tolerance. A half century after Postel, J. A. de Savigny in the *Discours sur les choses turques* (1606), which (as we have observed) was attributed to Georgievicz, stated that "those whom we call Turks are, for the most part, half-Christians and possibly closer to true Christianity than many among us."[71] William Bedwell, a distinguished mathematician and Arabist, whose refutation of Islam in the *Mohammedis Impostura* (London, 1615) gave evidence of much genuine learning, is said to have imported from Leyden the first font of Arabic type to be used in England. Despite the intention, announced in the sub-title to his book, to reveal the "horrible impieties of the blasphemous seducer Mohammed," his tone is not entirely immoderate in revealing Islam's debt to Christianity.[72]

Almost everywhere in Europe the Turks were filling the minds of nobles and peasants, seamen and intellectuals. As Albert Mas has shown, in the late sixteenth and earlier seventeenth centuries the Turks made a considerable impact upon the Spanish mind and spirit.[73] In fact, the Turks played a large part in Spanish historical studies, travel literature, novels, metrical romances, poetry, *comedias* in verse, "farces" dramatizing the Turks, etc., inspired by their successes at Constantinople (in 1453), Rhodes (1522–3), and elsewhere, and above all by their failures at Vienna (1529), Malta (1565), Lepanto (1571), and elsewhere, but especially by their failure at Lepanto. Italian works bearing upon *Turcica* were studied in the original texts as well as in those translated into Spanish.

---

erence to Georgievicz (p. 394); also Secret, "L'Émithologie [*sic*] de Guillaume Postel," in *Archivio di filosofia*, 1960, nos. 2–3, pp. 381–437, and "L'Herméneutique de Guillaume Postel," *ibid.*, 1963, no. 3, pp. 91–145, with the prefaces to Postel's second (Latin) translation of the cabalistic *Zohar.*

[71] Georgievicz (and de Savigny), *Discours*, etc., p. 88, cited by Atkinson, *Nouveaux Horizons*, p. 135.

[72] Note the sketch of Bedwell's life as given by Wm. Robertson Smith, in the *DNB*, II, 119–20.

[73] Albert Mas, *Les Turcs dans la littérature espagnole du Siècle d'Or*, 2 vols., Paris, 1967.

Cervantes (d. 1616) and the dramatist Lope de Vega (d. 1635) excelled in *les turqueries espagnoles*, sometimes mixing up the Turks with the Moors. Cervantes' personal experiences with the Turks and Moors had a very large influence on his work; he was wounded at Lepanto, the injury crippling his left arm. In 1575 Cervantes was captured by the Barbary pirates; he spent five years as a prisoner in Algiers, and was ransomed at a high price in 1580, when he returned to Spain. Lope de Vega, while he lacked Cervantes' depth of feeling when it came to the Turks, employed the *turqueries* as dramatic devices in brilliant fashion. A literary historian and critic of learning and acumen, Mas has explored every aspect of the Turks' influence upon the Spanish mind in the golden age of Spanish literature.

In 1625 Michel Baudier of Languedoc published in Paris his *Histoire générale de la religion des Turcs, avec la naissance, la vie et la mort de leur prophète Mahomet* (with re-editions in 1632, 1640, and 1741). Written on the anti-Islamic bias of the monkish literature of the middle ages, it supplied much fact as well as fancy. The learned notes accompanying the famous Edward Pococke's *Specimen historiae Arabum*, which appeared in 1650, extended the range of Arabic sources available to western scholars, and were later used by Prideaux and Gibbon. Thirteen years later (in 1663) Pococke published the Arabic text, with a Latin translation, of the *Historia compendiosa dynastiarum* of abū-l-Farāj (Bar Hebraeus), which had formed the core of his *Specimen*. Pococke was professor of Arabic (and later of Hebrew) at Oxford, and had spent more than five years at Aleppo (1630–1636) and almost three years in Istanbul (1637–1640). In 1806 Joseph White brought out a second edition of Pococke's *Specimen*, which was indeed an important work.[74]

---

[74] With numerous royalist connections, Edw. Pococke led an occasionally troubled life until the Restoration (in 1660), after which "he lived in studious ease at Christ Church [Oxford] in the lodgings of the Hebrew professor." One of the truly notable scholars of the seventeenth century, Pococke died at Oxford in his eighty-seventh year (in 1691). See the account of his life by Stanley Lane-Poole, in the *DNB*, XVI, 7–12.

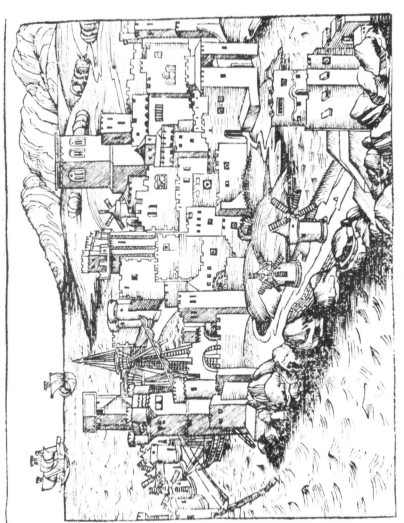

Rhodes

In 1647 André du Ryer, Sieur de Malezair, sometime French consul in Alexandria, published the first French translation of the Koran (*L'Alcoran de Mahomet*),[75] which was reprinted more than a half dozen times in the next century and a half, and despite its inaccuracies and inadequacies something of Mohammed's teachings was made directly available in a language which every educated European could read. Since the time of Francis I the French had had closer relations with the Porte than had any other western nation (although many Italians traded with and worked for the Turks), and of course in the later seventeenth and eighteenth centuries France (and England) exercised an intellectual dominance over Europe. It is now that we enter an era of persuasive rationalism, "enlightenment," which helped to sow the seeds of deism, often deviating into atheism. The deists were not generally given to prophecy, or were at least unlikely to take it seriously. If one could build mosques in western cities in the nineteenth century, it was largely owing to the rescue of Mohammed from medieval abuse by the historians, *philosophes*, dramatists, and (Protestant) theologians of the two preceding centuries, especially in France and England.

Blaise Pascal continued the Christian hostility to Islam in certain passages in his *Pensées*, however, and the Italian theologian and orientalist Fra Lodovico Marracci mounted a massive attack in his learned *Prodromus ad refutationem Alcorani* (Rome, 1691, reprinted at Padua, 1698) and his publication of the Arabic text of the Koran, *Alcorani textus universus . . .* (Padua, 1698), which was accompanied by a Latin translation with extensive notes and refutations. Marracci rejected the spurious legends, but the purpose of his work was clearly announced on his title page: *Mahumetus ipse gladio*

---

[75] The French text was put into English two years later (1649), possibly by Alexander Ross, who published with the translation "A Needful Caveat or Admonition," in which he excoriated Mohammed and attacked Islam although he was prepared to concede certain virtues to the Moslems (cf. B. P. Smith, *Islam in English Literature*, Beirut, 1939, pp. 26–28, and Chew, *The Crescent and the Rose*, pp. 448–51).

suo jugulatur.[76] Further refutations of Islam followed from
the pen of the English divine Humphrey Prideaux, dean of
Norwich, whose faulty work on *The True Nature of Impos-
ture Fully Display'd in the Life of Mahomet* (London, 1697)
was often reprinted and widely studied for more than a century. Prideaux's purpose was to defend Christianity against
the derogations of the deists, but he went back to Ricoldo da
Montecroce for many of his arguments.[77]

Progress was slowly being made in understanding Islam,
and much less than the common prejudice was shown by the
theologian Johann Heinrich Hottinger in his *Historia orien-
talis* (Zürich, 1651) and by Richard Simon, who wrote under
the pseudonym Sieur de Moni an *Histoire critique de la
créance et des coûtumes des nations du Levant* (Frankfurt,
1684). The work of rehabilitation was continued by Adrian
Reland, professor of oriental languages at Utrecht, in his
work *De religione mohammedica libri II* (Utrecht, 1705,
and soon followed by translations in English, French, and
German) as well as by Jean Gagnier in *Ismael Abu'l-Feda de
vita et rebus gestis Mohammedis* (Oxford, 1723) and the *Vie
de Mahomet* (Amsterdam, 1732), which tended to make
Mohammed almost a good Protestant and in any event a per-
ceptive enemy of the Curia Romana. Scholarship was slowly
freeing oriental history of anti-Moslem polemic. In 1734
George Sale's translation of the Koran appeared in London
(he owed much to the text and notes of Marracci); to his work
was prefixed a *Preliminary Discourse*, giving a summary of

---

[76] On Marracci's work, see especially the learned study of Carlo Alfonso Nallino, "Le Fonti arabe manoscritte dell' opera di Ludovico Marracci sul Corano," in the *Rendiconti della R. Accademia nazionale dei
Lincei, Cl. di scienze morali, storiche e filologiche*, 6th ser., VII (1931),
303–49. Marracci died in Rome in 1700, at eighty-eight years of age. As
Nallino reminds us (*op. cit.*, p. 349), the Turks laid siege to Vienna in 1683
while Marracci was engaged in the preparation of his *Prodromus* (1691),
which he dedicated to the emperor Leopold I, King John III Sobieski of
Poland, the Republic of Venice, and other Christian princes who (together
with the popes) "foedere iuncti arma sua Christo contra Mahumeticam
impietatem devovere."

[77] On Prideaux, "a man of more frankness than refinement of mind,"
cf. Alexander Gordon's account of his life and work in the *DNB*, XVI,
352–54.

Arabic religious history and a short life of Mohammed; and although Sale deplored the prophet's having imposed "a false religion on mankind," he was much less prejudiced against Islam than most of his predecessors.

The *philosophes* of the Enlightenment found a means of expressing their anti-clericalism and of attacking Catholicism by presenting Mohammed as a great religious leader, whose main objectives had been liberty, tolerance, and social justice, not apotheosis, as Count Henri de Boulainvilliers (d. 1722) explained in his posthumous work on *La Vie de Mahomed* (London and Amsterdam, 1730), which also appeared in English (1731) and German (1747) translations. To the Catholics Mohammed remained the arch-heretic; to the Protestants he became a misguided pastor. The *philosophes* professed to admire him not only as the tolerant founder of a new religion, but also as a great legislator and as a warrior statesman.

Throughout the eighteenth century Mohammed appeared both on the stage and in novels, especially amorous farces. Voltaire's tedious tragedy *Le Fanatisme ou Mahomet le Prophète* was written between 1739 and '42, and was dedicated to Pope Benedict XIV. Despite the wicked travesty of Mohammed, who is represented as a criminal charlatan, Voltaire's drama made the usual plea of the *philosophes* for freedom of expression and religion. Rome was thinly disguised as Mecca, and S. Ignatius Loyola was hinted at in the characterization of Mohammed. But Voltaire paid tribute to Mohammed, without liking him, in the *Essai sur les moeurs* as a powerful leader and in some measure the exponent of religious tolerance. The apostles of the Enlightenment took up the theme with an enthusiasm as historically benighted as the medieval denigration of the Prophet had been. Claude Savary brought out a new French translation of the Koran in 1783, to go with the new personality of Mohammed and the new concept of Islam.[78] Christian hostility was passing

---

[78] See in general Pierre Martino, "Mahomet en France au XVIIᵉ et au XVIIIᵉ siècle," *Actes du XIVᵉ Congrès International des Orientalistes* [*Alger, 1905*], pt. III (Paris, 1907), 206–41, and cf. also Martino, *L'Orient*

away as the Turcophobia receded, and Mohammed and the Moslems could be admired (or ridiculed) in an era when the Turk was becoming the sick man of Europe.

The Turks had not kept up with science and technology, and had failed entirely to enter the industrial revolution which was transforming Europe, where fear of the Turk was being replaced by impatience, contempt, and annoyance, especially among those who were seeking to wring profits from the Levant. For example (one among many), Christophe Aubin, an agent of the British commercial firm of J. Finlay and Company (of Glasgow), quickly acquired a jaundiced view of the Turks (in 1812) deciding, according to A. B. Cunningham, that "Turkey . . . was a land where there was too little justice, but too much of everything else—fires, plagues, wars, rebellions, and worthless coinage."[79]

In the East prophets continued to appear into the later nineteenth century, and are doubtless still active today. Although rather removed from the main theme of this article, let us note a last example. In the spring of 1874 a Jew named Bohor Levy, who was said to have made various accurate predic-

---

dans la littérature française au XVIIe et au XVIIIe siècle, Paris: Hachette, 1906, esp. pp. 133–38, 159–66, 173ff., 217–20, who seems to think that the historian of the Turks, "Chalcondyle," was a writer of the seventeenth century (p. 135, note 1) and that Anastasius [Bibliothecarius] was a Byzantine monk (p. 161, note 1). Actually Blaise de Vigenère's French translation of the late fifteenth-century work of the Greek historian Laonicus [Nicolaos] Chalcocondylas first appeared in Paris in 1577, and was reprinted in 1584 (Bibl. Nationale, J. 3,290–91). On the gradual diminution of the western prejudice against Islam, cf. also Daniel, *Islam and the West*, pp. 283–301.

As for the almost everlasting conflict between East and West, as reflected in the modern novel, see Issa J. Boullata, "Encounter between East and West: A Theme in Contemporary Arabic Novels," *The Middle East Journal*, XXX (1976), 49–62; on the American assumption "that the Arab stance is hostile towards the West" (owing partly to the confusion of Iranians [Persians] with Arabs), note Shelley Slade, "The Image of the Arab in America: Analysis of a Poll on American Attitudes," *ibid.*, XXXV (1981), 143–62; and on the Islamic "rejection of the West," cf. Yvonne Yazbeck Haddad, "The Qur'anic Justification for an Islamic Revolution . . .," *ibid.*, XXXVII (1983), esp. pp. 24–29.

[79] Cunningham, "The Journal of Christophe Aubin: A Report on the Levant Trade in 1812," *Archivum Ottomanicum*, VIII (1983), 14.

tions, kept the people of Istanbul in a state of constant excitement by a prophecy that during the night of 8–9 June the Christian resort town of Kadiköy, the ancient Chalcedon, would be destroyed. The earth, he was represented as saying, would open up and swallow the town. Panic seized the inhabitants of Kadiköy, many of whom left the area to seek safety elsewhere. In a police investigation Bohor Levy denied having made any such prediction. Although this reassuring news was published, and Kadiköy was not swallowed up by an earthquake, there was more to his prediction than could be learned from contemporary newspaper accounts.

Some years later the German Turcologist Johann Heinrich Mordtmann (d. 1932) received further details of Bohor Levy's prediction from a high official of the Porte. Actually the prophet was said to have foretold that "something which begins with the letter *Kāf* [K], will be swallowed up," which the inhabitants of Kadiköy took to mean their town. Fearful people sold their property, which a certain Haronaji bought up at ridiculously low prices, and it was later assumed that the prophet and the purchaser were accomplices in a swindle. But there was reason to doubt this when on the night of 19–20 June (1874) the steamer Kars, which also "began with the letter *Kāf*," collided with an Egyptian steamer and sank in the Sea of Marmara as it set out for Thessaloniki. The meaning of Bohor Levy's prediction thus became clear, and Mordtmann's informant was quite convinced that the Jewish seer did indeed have the gift of prophecy. The Jews, he said, could inherit the gift from their forefathers,[80] and if this was the opinion of a high official of the Turkish government, it was obviously shared by many others of less education, notably by the inhabitants of Kadiköy.

If the Turks sometimes believed in the inspired art of prognostication, prophecy more than once beset them in the "twice ten years" from the Crimean to the Russo-Turkish War (1856–1876), and even in the West there were those who

---

[80] J. H. Mordtmann, "Alte und neue Propheten im Orient," *Mitteilungen des Seminars für Orientalische Sprachen . . . zu Berlin*, XXXIII (1930), pt. II: *Westasiatische Studien*, pp. 194–95.

awaited fulfillment of a prophecy that foretold the final dis-
solution of the Porte:

> In twice two hundred years the Bear
>   The Crescent shall assail
> But if the Cock and Bull unite,
>   The Bear shall not prevail.

> But look! in twice ten years again,
>   Let Islam know and fear,
> The Cross shall wax—the Crescent wane,
>   Grow pale and disappear.[81]

---

[81] This prophecy, even attributed by the gullible to Nostradamus
(1503–1566), is discussed in an interesting letter to *The Observer*, London,
28 November, 1915, by Mr. Henry Morris, who notes that Nostradamus predicted seven bloody changes in English history in 290 years, extending (presumably) from 1649 to 1939! For the prophecy, cf. Theophilus de Garen-
cières, *The True Prophecies or Prognostications of Michael Nostradamus*,
London, 1672, p. 128: Century III, no. LVII:

> Sept fois changer verrez gens Britanique,
> Teints en sang en deux cens nonante an . . .

This "prediction," however, of the outbreak of the Second World War loses
its effect when one considers Nostradamus' next verse:

> France non point par appuy Germanique . . .

France, that is, will not suffer the same bloody changes as England "because of German support!" Nostradamus, in his Century IV, no. IV (*op.
cit.*, p. 152) refers to the French as Cocks (*Coqs*), as in the nineteenth-
century prophecy given above (and cf. Century V, no. XIV, p. 198). The
Rev. Samuel Bush of New York, who wrote a *Life of Mohammed* (1830),
foresaw the end of both the papacy and Islam as coming in the year 1866
(B. P. Smith, *Islam in English Literature,* pp. 150–51).

Index

Vanli Effendi, later 17th century Turkish preacher, 37, (fn) 39
Varna, Turkish victory at (1444), 10
Venice, Republic of, 15, 24, 36, 49
Verdino of Otranto, Abbot (fl. 1594), 36
Vienna, Hapsburg imperial capital in Austria, on the Danube, 25, 51
Vincent of Beauvais (ca. 1190–ca. 1264), Dominican encyclopedist, 4, 49

Voltaire, François Marie Arouet de (b. 1694, d. 1778), 55
Wagner, Tobias (b. 1598, d. 1680), Lutheran preacher, 41
Wendt, Michael, printer (fl. 1663), 41
White, Joseph, published second edition of Pococke's *Specimen* (1806), 52
Zagreb [Agram], capital of Croatia, 29
Zeno, Antonio, provost, church of Volterra (early 16th century), 23